"Ken Fortier has written an extraordinary book, which anyone—especially those in sales and marketing—should be required to read in order to determine if they are more of a 'NetPlus' or a 'NetMinus' person.

"But I would also recommend that you look at the difference between the two more as a spectrum than two absolute states, and ask yourself, "Where do I fall along this spectrum?" and, "What could I do to move my dial towards being more of an ideal 'NetPlus' person—in business as well as in my personal and family life?"

— Bob Littell
Chief NetWeaver and CEO of The Enrichment Company and NetWeaving International, past President of the Pay It Forward Foundation, and author of *Power NetWeaving,* the *The Heart and Art of NetWeaving,* and *Raising Your R&R Factor: How Referable and Recommendable Are You?*

NetPlus Connections

Make Everyone Else's World Bigger and Better

Ken Fortier

with Greg Smith

Black Lake Press
TELL YOUR STORY
BLACKLAKEPRESS.COM

Cover design by Greg Smith of Black Lake Studio.

Published by Black Lake Press of Holland, Michigan.
Black Lake Press is a division of Black Lake Studio, LLC.
Direct inquiries to Black Lake Press at
www.blacklakepress.com.

ISBN 978-0-9839602-4-9

Dedication

Barbie, I appreciate you and your love for me during this very exciting time. You inspire me to be better, and I'm honored to share my life with you! Jake and Kaitlyn, go after your dreams! Cherish and develop all the connections in your life and know that I will be here for you forever!

Mom and Dad, thank you for your love, discipline and support these past forty-four years! My gift to you is my commitment to never give up, to stay loving and committed to my family and strive to be an example to all like you have been for me. I love you both!

Olivia Shea, my niece and Brendan Florido, my friend thank you for your titles, drawings and quotes! I appreciate and love you both!

Table of Contents

Value Attracts Value

Acknowledgements

Thank you Barbie, for your love and encouragement! I love and appreciate you so much!

Thank you Dan and Juanita Fortier, my parents for your inspiration and support these past 44 years!

Thank you Jake and Kaitlyn for your trust in me and your commitment to being your best always!

Thank you to the team at Black Lake Studio and Press. Thanks to Greg Smith for his time and creativity, helping me to develop and write *Netplus Connections*. Thanks to Mike Dokter and Rob Stam for their commitment, time, and energy pulling together and promoting NetPlus. Thanks to Sam Tzou and Linda Smith for their editorial expertise and efforts.

Thank you to Sally Heavener, Tim Dyer, and Richard Wroten for reading the rough draft and their constructive feedback.

Thank you Jason Madden, Cathy Rogg and Davenport University. Your generosity and promotion for the launch was remarkable! I am so proud to be an alumni of DU and am honored to be included in such an elite group of Alumni.

Thank you Bob Tobin for being such a great mentor and friend. From the days when you coached me in eighth grade basketball until now you have always been a true NetPlus person in my life.

Thank you Fred Cook for your leadership and friendship. I appreciate you and it's been a pleasure to become close friends with your family, James, Tom, Freddy Jr. and Elaine.

Thank you Fathers Tom Donaldson and Danielson, and Tom Wouldstra, for always being there for me.

Thank you Bob Littel for your inspiration and your Netweaving philosophy. It's given an identity to what I enjoy doing and teaching and is the foundation to *NetPlus Connections*.

Thank you Wendy Dejong and the team at Gilson Graphics for your fast and impressive work printing *NetPlus Connections!*

Thank you to my entire team at Quantum Leap Communications for your commitment and trust in our team!

Thank you Scott Goss for your support and leadership in my life.

Thank you Ron Alvesteffor for sharing your vision with me and my team! NetPlus is your middle name!

Thank you Bruce Pienton, "the God Father," your leadership and graciousness continues to inspire me.

Thank you Don Klein for your brilliance in combining your abilities in being an entrepreneur and trusted tax advisor.

Thank you Sally Heavener for being in my life you've always made my world bigger and better!

Thank you Mike and Vicki Micallef you are amazing friends and were there in our infancy to guide us on the right and best path for our business!

And last but NOT least thank you to "the boys:" Don Hamilton, Dennis Newton, Joe Klooster, Chris Wangler, Tom Stritzinger, Chris Nawrocki, Tim Dyer and my bro Jimmy Fortier. Since grade school, through high school, in our amazing college days to present, I hope you realize how much of an impact you have made in my life please know I will always be your friend.

Introduction

Make Their World
Bigger and Better

Facebook friends are not really friends, Twitter followers are not really followers, and you aren't really linked to anyone through LinkedIn. Although those tools may be as much a normal part of business today as Rolodexes and the Yellow Pages were a generation or so ago, they are not genuine professional relationships. Human connections are an essential (meaning "necessary," not just important) element of business activity, and the electronic age hasn't chipped away at their significance. Ever since the first humans traded a sharpened stick for a caribou skin, business connections have essentially been human relationships. We need to know someone to evaluate their potential, their trustworthiness, and their compatibility with our organization.

Over the last ten years, technology has helped us to increase the quantity of our connections, but not the quality. In fact, the quality of our professional relationships has suffered, as technology has encouraged superficial interaction. And while our behaviors have changed, the business needs have stayed the same. We still need to know people to trust them, to figure out how to work with them, and to understand how to connect them to others. That means engaging with them in face-to-face encounters, and forging alliances through shared experiences. The point is to learn who they are, and what the two of you can do for each other.

Business technology emphasizes the quantity of our business relationships, but not the quality

---

And that is where this book comes in. Too much of our business technology emphasizes the quantity of our business relationships, but not the quality. We try to get more eyeballs on our page or profile, have the eyeballs go wide with admiration at the cleverness of our branding, and then "click through" to us. But what then? What happens when they meet us in person? If we have not improved the quality of our business connections, the quantity doesn't help us. It is like the old joke about losing a little bit on every transaction, but making it up in volume. If our business relationship skills are bad, then all the networking techniques in the world only multiply our dysfunction, and we end up with lots of bad business relationships. But I believe that if we are good at building professional relationships, we will get many more, if for no other reason than because doors will be opened to meet exponentially more people. And if we have the skills to capitalize on those opportunities, then the sky is the limit.

If our business relationship skills are bad, then all the networking techniques in the world only multiply our dysfunction, and we end up with lots of bad business relationships

---

The purpose of NetPlus Connections is to help you to become as valuable of a connection as you can be to everyone that you meet and do business with. In fact, I want every one of your business connections to consider you an asset, someone that they are glad to have in their contact list, and someone they want to engage with as much as possible. I want them to consider you well-worth any time, money, or energy they spend on you. I want them to consider you so valuable that they want to introduce you to their other connections, so their friends can have the benefit of knowing and working with you as well.

The key to being this sort of valuable asset is simple: make everyone else's world bigger and better. Be a gateway to other people, ideas, solutions, and opportunities. Deliver such value in everything you do for other people that you are more than worth everything you cost them. It's just that simple: if you are worth more than you cost, you are a net asset. If you cost more than you are worth, then you are a net liability. Assets get protected and invested in, liabilities get dropped.

Be more than worth what you cost, and you will have all the connections and business you can handle

---

Before you read further, a word of warning. This is not a book full of techniques or tools to meet more contacts or drive more sales. I promise you, if you are an asset, then your world will get bigger and better—including your financial bottom line. But if you treat your contacts as just contacts, and your engagement with them as just sales, they will not consider you an asset. You might get their money, if they need you badly enough, but not their respect and loyalty. But over the long run, valuable, respected professionals who have the loyalty of their customers and colleagues also get financially rewarded.

Be worth more than what you cost, and you will have all the connections and business you can handle. This book will teach you how.

• • •

"The most important single ingredient in the formula of success is knowing how to get along with people."
— Theodore Roosevelt

Part I
Relational Accounting

connections

chapter 1

Relational Balance Sheets

Though most of us would never admit it, even to ourselves, we all have what might be called a "relational balance sheet." You may never have thought of it in these terms, but whether consciously or subconsciously, you evaluate what people give you, and subtract what they cost you. Liabilities are subtracted from assets, producing a bottom line, just like a financial balance sheet in a business. When all the adding and subtracting is done, there is a bottom line. Either that person costs you more than they are worth to you, or is worth more than they cost you. The former is a "net liability" (or a "net minus"), and the latter is a "net asset" (or "net plus").

Let me give you the easiest possible example. Suppose you own a business, and have a salesperson working for you. You pay the salesperson a salary, plus other costs such as benefits, employer taxes, the employees workspace, phone and computers, support staff, expenses in the field, etc. Those are the liabilities. You then total up how much of your product or service they sell in a month, quarter or year. You subtract the costs from the revenue, and get a bottom line: are they a net plus asset, or a net minus liability?

Or consider your time. Let's suppose that you have a colleague who likes to meet with you. Lunch meetings, coffee meetings, text messages, invitations to events, etc. Your time is limited; in fact, we all have the exact same amount of finite time: twenty-four hours per day. This colleague is costing you time that you could be spending on something else: other business associates, your family, personal interests, sleeping, exercising, or reading a book. However, that investment of time in your colleague might be producing some good results: work product, ideas, connections to other people and opportunities, the satisfaction of helping someone in need, etc. But when you subtract the amount of time you spend on them from the outcomes it produces, is that relationship a net plus asset for you, or a net minus?

We could say the same thing about emotional investment, mental energy, relationships with other people, etc. In fact, throughout this book we're going to conveniently describe all of these costs as "opportunities and resources." Our resources are time, money, mental and emotional energy, materials, and so on.

But there are also opportunity costs to every action we take: if we choose action A, we can't choose action B. A has to be worth more than what B would have been to make A worth the choice. And so, the hour we spend with someone doesn't just cost us the hour. It costs us all of the other things we could have done with that hour. The same thing is true for money, energy, materials, etc. But opportunities are not just other ways we could have spent our resources, they are other possibilities we could have pursued.

When I add up what opportunities and resources I spend on you, and subtract them from the opportunities and resources that you provide me, you become either a NetPlus person on my balance sheet, or a NetMinus.

For example, let's say that you are a contractor who does home remodeling projects, and I have a good friend who just bought a new house and wants to have some work done. You want me to introduce you to my friend. That's an opportunity for you, but that opportunity has a cost for me: what if you do a bad job, and my friend resents me sending him a bad contractor? And what about the other three contractors that I know? If I personally endorse you to my friend, how will that impact my relationship with him? How might my helping you to get a job working on my friend's house impact my relationship with you? What if I would prefer for our relationship to remain as it is?

When I add up what opportunities and resources I spend on you, and subtract them from the opportunities and resources that you provide me, you become either a NetPlus person on my balance sheet, or a NetMinus. There are three fundamental premises to this book:

1. Relational accounting is real. Whether we admit it to ourselves or not, we all do this.

2. We enjoy and invest in the NetPlus people in our lives, while we resent and pull away from the NetMinuses.

3. We should strive to be a NetPlus person, to be worth more than we cost, to everyone around us.

Before you object to thinking of human relationships in such selfish terms, hear me out. First, there are all sorts of intangible benefits to some relationships. Some people might cost you time and money, but investing in them might bring you joy, satisfaction, even pleasure. Mentoring a young colleague, serving in a charity, tutoring a struggling child, coaching a youth sports team, going on a mission trip through your church, serving on a committee at school, caring for an elderly person—all of these might give you back far more than they cost you in opportunities and resources. That child that you tutor or senior citizen that you take meals to might be the most NetPlus person on your balance sheet, and spur you to invest even more with them, or similar relationships.

There are all sorts of intangible benefits to some relationships. Some people might cost you time and money, but investing in them might bring you joy, satisfaction, even pleasure.

Second, this book focuses on professional relationships. While I think that the principle holds true in all human relationships, we all love our family (or should), and gladly give our lives for them without expectation of return. Whatever my family costs me in time, money, energy, opportunities, and everything else, I get far more back in love, joy, and the deep, soul-satisfying knowledge that I am serving and investing in the ones I love. Caring for a baby may take a lot out of us, but none of us regrets that investment for a moment.

Develop your professional character so that you are valuable to everyone who does business with you. Worry less about where other people sit on your balance sheet, and more about where you sit on theirs. Go through your career being worth far more than you cost.

Finally, we have moral and ethical obligations to serve others. In fact, one of the qualities of a NetPlus person is how he or she treats those who can do nothing for them in return. But we do not have an obligation to spend all our opportunities and resources on everyone we meet, endlessly and thoughtlessly. One of the first rules for any search and rescue team is not to endanger themselves in the course of the rescue, otherwise they might create more victims that need to be rescued. We have a moral and ethical obligation to be good stewards of our opportunities and resources. If I spend a dollar or an hour helping someone in need, I didn't help someone else. Sometimes, I need to spontaneously give and not worry about the outcome. But sometimes, I need to spend my charity wisely, in a way that has the greatest possible impact. And I also need to maintain my other commitments, so that I will have another dollar and another hour next week to share with someone in need.

Let me conclude with an important point: this book is not really about finding and rejecting NetMinus people. It is about being a NetPlus person to those around you. This book is about developing your professional character so that you are valuable to everyone who does business with you. Worry less about where other people sit on your balance sheet, and more about where you sit on theirs.

The NetPlus strategy is to go through your career being worth far more than you cost. The result is success for everyone, including you.

• • •

"The greatest ability in business is to get along with others and influence their actions. A chip on the shoulder is too heavy a piece of baggage to carry through life."
— John Hancock

chapter 2

Qualities of NetPlus People

Strictly defined, anyone is a net plus on your balance sheet if they are worth more to you than they cost you. But NetPlus professionals, people that you do business with who are net assets on your balance sheet, share some common traits. I have seen these patterns play out over the years in every industry I am familiar with, and in people of every generation or race. These are basic characteristics of professional relationships, whether they be with colleagues, clients, contractors, or coworkers. They apply to bosses and employees. NetPlus people don't necessarily score equally on all of these qualities, of course, but they do well on enough of them to be in the positive column with me. And NetMinus people don't necessarily fail all of these criteria, but the sum total brings them up short.

Qualities of NetPlus People:

• Are Genuinely Grateful.

• Raise My Energy Level.

• Understand My Needs.

• Solve Problems, Not Create Them.

• Don't Complain Much.

• Connect Me to Other NetPlus People.

• Don't Divide or Drive Away Others.

• Are Connected to Other Fields.

• Know Where to Go for Solutions, Ideas, and Opportunities.

• Teach Me Useful Things.

---

1. NetPlus People Are Genuinely Grateful.

Gratitude is not a behavior, it is a character trait. Grateful people don't just say thank you, or send a nice note, or return a favor. Those behaviors can be signs of gratitude, but they might also be insincere social conventions, or even attempts to flatter and manipulate. Genuine gratitude is a condition of the heart. It comes from a humble acknowledgement that while we deserve what we earn through achievement and hard work, our native gifts and abilities come from God, and were cultivated by parents, teachers, pastors, priests, and coaches. It recognizes that we were given opportunities along the way through our career, and that we are blessed by the time and place that we live. Grateful people have happy and optimistic outlooks, because they are thankful for what they have, rather than resenting what they don't have. On the other hand, grateful people do not have a sense of entitlement; they don't believe that others owe them anything more than courtesy and whatever they've earned by merit. A sense of entitlement kills a thankful heart because it believes that it deserves whatever it wants. It can't acknowledge gifts and opportunities, and resents the genuine achievement of others.

NetMinus People Take More Than They Give in Relationships.

They don't just cost more on my balance sheet, they are takers and users who actively subtract from it. They feel entitled to my opportunities and resources, and feel no gratitude for what God or other people have given them. They are are not optimistic and are rarely happy, because they are focused on what they don't have, and resent what others have received.

2. NetPlus People Raise My Energy Level.

I feel better when I am around NetPlus people. I feel positive, confident, courageous, optimistic, imaginative, and energetic. They make me feel like a better person, and make me want to be a even better person yet. I perform at a higher level when they are around, and after I spend time with them I feel like I can do great things.

But these people can be very different from each other, and have this effect on me in different ways. Some make me laugh, some make me think, some inspire me by their example, some give me pep talks. Some have achieved more in their careers, and some less. Some are business people, some work in education, or the church, or sports and entertainment. Some are friends or family, and some are people I don't know well, but I would like to get to know better. But the common denominator is the effect they have on me. Most of them don't realize that they are doing it, and none are trying to do so. It just flows naturally out of who they are.

NetMinus People Make Make Me Feel Tired, Depressed, Angry, or Frightened.

Like the people who make me feel great, most of the people who make me feel bad, or miserable, don't realize that they are doing it. Almost none of them are trying to have this effect on me. Like the NetPlus people, this negativity naturally flows out of who they are. They suck energy with their words, their attitudes, their demeanors, and their behaviors. They always see the dark side of every situation, dwell on problems and suffering, are angry about all sorts of things, imagine worst-case scenarios, and forecast bad outcomes. Sometimes, their analysis or predictions are correct, but the way they frame the issues makes the situation worse than it has to be. An hour or two with someone like this wipes me out emotionally for the rest of the day.

3. NetPlus People Understand My Needs.

Some people "get it" without having it explained to them: the salesperson who figures out and proposes the right solution for my problem, the employee who sees what my business needs and handles it without being asked, the coach who knows what I'm doing wrong and how to help me improve my game, the real estate agent who knows just the right house for my family. I may be fixated on my wants, or unable to articulate my ideas, but NetPlus people usually understand what I need better than I do. They zero in on the real problem, and know how to solve it.

The tools NetPlus people use to zero in on my needs are listening, intuition, and experience. They are emotionally intelligent, and don't just pay attention to what I'm saying, but discover the issues that lie behind my words. They know how to read between the lines, and see the bigger picture. Most of all, they are intent on understanding my needs, rather than waiting for an opportunity to change the subject to theirs.

NetMinus People, If They Help At All, Give Me What They Want to Give, Not What I Need.

A NetMinus salesperson doesn't figure out what I need, he pushes what he's selling. A NetMinus employee doesn't volunteer for what needs to be done, but for what they want to do. A NetMinus colleague doesn't introduce me to the people I need to meet, but to the people he wants to promote. NetMinus people always leave me stuck with something that I didn't want, my original need still unmet, and wondering how the time was wasted.

4. NetPlus People Solve Problems, Not Create Them.

Quite simply, NetPlus people fix things that are broken and don't break things that work. NetPlus people know how to diagnose symptoms, whether it is a machine that isn't working right, a client that is unhappy, or a department that is underperforming. They don't get rattled or frustrated. They stick with it until they figure out the underlying cause. While the people around them only see the consequences of the problem and get stuck in a loop of frustration, blame, and pessimism, NetPlus people see options and possibilities and start working to bring them about. Whether it is a conflict, a lost delivery, a cancelled flight, or lost data, they shrug and begin untangling the mess. While other people may leave messes behind them—interpersonal, financial, organizational—NetPlus people don't create problems. They take the time to clean up the loose ends on their own initiative, not leaving me extra work to do. I never have to worry about NetPlus people when they are in charge or operating on their own. They get things done.

NetMinus People Seem to Create Problems Wherever They Go.

NetMinus people turn the ordinary adversities of life into extraordinary difficulties. A flight cancelled because of the weather becomes a crisis that ruins a business deal. A difference of opinion on the team leads to someone quitting. An email is forwarded to someone it should not have been, leading to another lost client. Projects are always behind schedule and over budget. They exaggerate and force everyone around them to overreact. Times and places and names and dates are always jumbled up, causing confusion. You spend most of your time putting out fires they either started and or couldn't put out themselves.

5. NetPlus People Don't Complain Much.

I already said that NetMinus people lower my energy level with negativity, but often that arises from their attitude. Complaining is a specific behavior, and NetPlus people don't do it very often. To be fair, even the most positive people will occasionally tell the waiter that their food wasn't cooked as they requested, or complain to customer service if their reservation was lost. But persistent complaining, keeping a list of gripes and vocalizing them to anyone who listens, is not NetPlus behavior. Nor is excessively railing on someone who can't do anything about your problem. For example, I have seen grown business executives, supposedly mature and successful, bellow and whine like spoiled children at an airline gate attendant because of a weather delay. The snow is falling outside, the planes are sitting on the tarmac, and a man is practically yelling at some young woman, demanding that she do something. What? She can't cancel the storm. I've traveled with colleagues who complained about the weather, complained about the flight, complained about the food, complained about the rental car, complained about the hotel, complained about the conference or client, complained about the cellular phone coverage. I was embarrassed to be traveling with them, and won't next time. In contrast, I'm never embarrassed to travel—or do anything else—with a NetPlus person.

NetMinus People See Themselves as Victims.

The complaining arises, I think, from their perception of themselves as victims. They see the world as out to get them. While the flight was just delayed because of weather, in their mind the airline screwed them. The hotel, or restaurant, or rental car company ripped them off. The conference or client wasted their time. In their mind, everyone and everything is an adversary, and they go through life being taken advantage of. They are passive, being acted on by dark forces beyond their control. Anything that goes wrong is someone else's fault, and probably intentional. It is very difficult to work with someone like this, much less spend time with them. They become NetMinus in my column very quickly, and I avoid investing my opportunities and resources in them. They will only find fault and blame me for something in the end.

6. NetPlus People Connect Me to Other Net-Plus People.

NetPlus people make my world bigger because they are gateways to other valuable professionals. NetPlus people are connectors: they not only know other quality individuals, they introduce them to each other. Because my NetPlus friends are net assets to those around them, their contact lists are not only long, but full of smart, interesting, successful people who value and stay in touch with them. They can make a call or send an email, and get me an introduction to someone that will be valuable to me. We'll talk about this at length in the second section of this book, *Make Their World Bigger*.

NetMinus People Don't Make Connections for Me At All, Or If They Do, It Is To Other Net-Minus People.

NetMinus people don't have a lot of connections. Their professional world is not very large. They may have met and worked with a lot of people, but they don't have access to them because they are NetMinus, and people have pulled back from investing in them. The relationships that they do have are mostly with other NetMinus people, who share their negativity and dysfunctional behaviors. NetMinus people keep adding to my expenses: they cost me opportunities and resources, and they are always introducing me to others who will be a further drain. I never let NetMinus people recruit for a team or hire new employees: they attract others with their mindset and behaviors. Because of their insecurities, NetMinuses don't recruit or hire NetPluses, they surround themselves with NetMinuses *who are weaker than they are*. This rots an organization from within.

7. NetPlus People Don't Divide or Drive Away Others.

NetPlus people have people skills. They build coalitions, smooth ruffled feathers, inspire loyalty, and encourage teamwork. They don't always fall for groupthink, and support individual initiative. But they know how to keep egos in check—theirs and those around them—so that people keep working together toward a common goal. They don't let personal agendas or personal problems divide people, and they don't let anyone get mad and quit the process. They get more done, if for no other reason than that their time and energy isn't wasted on squabbles and spats. They can defuse a situation, so that opportunities aren't lost because of pointless conflicts.

NetMinus People Shrink My Contact List.

NetMinus people create conflicts where none existed. They escalate existing differences. They manage to drive wedges between people, and cause meetings and relationships to blow up. There is always turnover in a team, or on the client list. They alienate others, and don't get invited back to events. This is usually unintentional. Not even NetMinus people want to cause people problems. But they lack the skills to manage people and keep small differences small. Often, the harder they try to "fix" a situation with people, the worse the situation becomes. They manage to step on every mine in the minefield. As a result, I lose clients and colleagues due to their interpersonal bungling.

8. NetPlus People are Connected to Other Fields.

NetPlus people have open minds. Although they are competent and connected in their field, they are curious about the bigger world around them. They are lifelong learners, and seek out and participate in things that expand their horizons. A NetPlus engineer might be interested in cooking, and knows all the good restaurants in town. A NetPlus salesperson might have traveled extensively and have interesting insights on all sorts of issues. Rather than being irrelevant to their coworkers or clients, NetPlus people have larger bases of knowledge, and can call on more experiences. They have broader perspectives, and often come up with unique solutions. They see things that other people, who have a more narrow focus, miss.

NetMinus People Are Not Interested In Anything Outside Of Their Own Narrow Field Of Self-Interest.

NetMinus people are not broadly curious, because they are obsessed with themselves and their own problems and needs. They may be an expert in their field, but only in their field. They are not lifelong learners who seek out new ideas and new technologies. They might be the smartest person in the room, and might know more about the subject at hand than anyone else there, but they often miss opportunities because they cannot see the issue from any other angles.

9. NetPlus People Know Where to Go for Solutions, Ideas, and Opportunities.

Because NetPlus people are broadly curious about the world around them and knowledgeable in other fields, they have sources for new ideas, solutions to problems, or opportunities that those around them didn't know about. NetPlus people are connectors, so they have more relationships with people and organizations than the more narrowly focused NetMinuses.

If I need a contractor or consultant who can do something that I don't know how to do, a NetPlus doesn't resort to Googling for help, because they either know the right person, or they know someone who does. If I am looking for new suppliers or new markets, the NetPlus has good ideas, and probably has leads or contacts with leads. NetPlus people don't just have a long contact list, but for any given problem they probably "know a guy" (or a company) who can help with what I need.

NetMinus People Don't Know Where To Find Solutions, Ideas, or Opportunities.

NetMinus people not only have smaller professional worlds, their worlds are remarkably unproductive. They are self-contained, and have no doors out. They haven't cultivated the kind of helpful, reciprocal relationships that produce solutions on the fly. Because they are rarely curious, adventurous, or interested in anything other than themselves, they have not explored the world enough to know how to discover new people and ideas when they have to. Because they are NetMinus, they may know a lot guys, but have never invested enough in quality connections to "know a guy."

10. NetPlus People Teach Me Useful Things.

I want to be a lifelong learner. As soon as I stop learning, I stop being useful to others and competitive in my business. I love NetPlus people because I always learn things from them. Most of the NetPlus people I know are smarter than I am, or at least are experts in things that I am not. They are generous in sharing suggestions, ideas, and solutions. If I tell them, or see, that I have some challenge, they don't just solve my problem, they teach me to solve it next time. They also don't wait for me to ask them for help, or for ideas. They are born teachers. Maybe not in the classroom sense, but they are always teaching by illustration and example. To spend time with a NetPlus person—at an event, riding in a car, or sharing a cup of coffee—is to be always learning something. They might share a story about their business, but if I pay attention, they are modeling or teaching me a solution or method. I often will jot down what they told me, or call them afterward to ask for more detail if I'm dealing with a similar situation.

NetMinus People Give Me Information, But Not Useful Knowledge.

NetMinus people also lecture, instruct, write endless emails, and tell me about what they are up to. But it's usually just information. NetMinus people lack the empathy, curiosity, and judgment to understand what would be useful to me. While the NetPlus person intuitively (I doubt that they really think about it) shares relevant ideas in conversation, the NetMinus is so focused on himself that he can only talk about what interests him. It is rarely practical or valuable for me.

• • •

"This is the true joy in life: being used for a purpose recognized by yourself as a mighty one; being thoroughly worn out before you are thrown on the scrap heap; being a force of nature instead of a feverish selfish little clod of ailments and grievances complaining that the world will not devote itself to making you happy."
— George Bernard Shaw

chapter 3

Which Are You?

You (either consciously or subconsciously) evaluate your colleagues, deciding whether they are either net assets or net minuses to you. But (of course), they are doing the same thing to you. When they see an email from you in their inbox, or you coming from across the room at an event, or your name on the caller ID on their phone, they are deciding how much of their time, opportunities, and resources they want to invest in you in the coming moments.

Are you a NetPlus or NetMinus to the individuals that you work or associate with? Set this book down for a few minutes and open the professional contact list on your computer or phone. Run down the names, and ask yourself whether each person there currently considers you an asset to their professional life. It actually might take more than a few minutes, because I guarantee that if you really reflect on that question, you will be surprised by some of the conclusions you come to. There will be some people who are assets to you, but might not feel the same way about you. Conversely, there will be some people that annoy you, or you might outright avoid, but who value you immensely. Make a simple, two column list: people who consider you a NetPlus asset to their professional life, and those who consider you a NetMinus. Put all of your contacts into one of these two columns. I really encourage you to take the time to do this exercise. It will be eye-opening, and maybe even a little uncomfortable.

When you look at the two columns, which has more names in it? All of us are a NetMinus to someone because we have different interests, personalities, etc. But if the above list indicates that you think more of your contacts consider you NetMinus than NetPlus, then you have become aware of a pattern. Your attitudes and behaviors are limiting your career.

Self-awareness is the foundation of maturity, and the gateway to change. It can be painful, but you cannot grow unless you honestly understand who you are. How much is it costing you to not be honest with yourself. Are you willing to risk some painful reflection in order to become a more valuable and successful professional? If so, ask yourself the following questions:

Self-Assessment Exercise

1. Take a sheet of paper, or a spreadsheet, and make two columns

2. Go through your contact list or address book

3. For each name, honestly ask yourself, "Does this person consider me a NetPlus or NetMinus connection?"

4. Why?

5. Place each name in one of the two columns

6. Which list is longer? How is this affecting your career?

7. Reflect on any patterns you see in yourself. Ask yourself the questions in this chapter.

---

1. How are you at giving and receiving?

Let's start with receiving: are you genuinely grateful? I'm not asking if you are polite and say thank you, I'm asking if you truly feel thanksgiving in your heart for the life that you have, the opportunities you've been given, and the people who have invested in you. Or, deep down, do you feel like you deserve everything that you have? Or that you are entitled to it all? Because if you feel entitled, then you probably are taking other people and what they invest in you for granted. Even worse, you probably resent what you haven't gotten, or what those around you have received.

Grateful hearts remember the kindnesses and opportunities that others have invested in them, while ungrateful hearts can recount—in exquisite detail—every way they imagine that they were screwed over. If you have this sort of ungrateful heart, I guarantee that it is bubbling up to the surface, no matter how many polite thank you notes you send, and it is poisoning your business and career. It is making you a NetMinus person.

Gratitude is the source of giving. When we are grateful for how we have been treated, it overflows into how we treat others.

Gratitude is the source of giving. When we are grateful for how we have been treated, it overflows into how we treat others. People who have been given breaks in their career tend to give breaks to others. Those who have been mentored mentor others. Those who remember what it was like to need a hand tend to lend a hand.

If you want to understand why people consider you NetPlus or NetMinus, start by asking how you receive, and whether you give more than you demand, in your professional relationships.

2. Do you bring people up, or down?

It can be hard to see yourself through someone else's eyes. Do they find your stories interesting or your jokes funny, or are they only being polite when they listen or laugh? When they tell you that they enjoyed spending time with you, was it because they have good manners, or because you picked up the tab, or because they want you to sign their contract?

On the other hand, don't overanalyze it. What is your intuition say? Do you believe that you raise their energy level? Do they leave you feeling more positive? Do they initiate contact when they don't have to? Do they go out of their way to spend time with you? Do they enthusiastically introduce you to their best contacts, or include you in their activities?

And, looking back on your interactions, and be honest: are your conversations positive, encouraging, and interesting? When you speak, is it mostly complaints, criticisms, and caustic remarks?

3. Do you listen well, understand what people need, and give them that?

Some people think they are helping, but what they offer isn't what I need. Usually, it is what they wanted to give me, for their own reasons. Maybe it is what they would like to receive themselves, or is something that actually helps them more than me.

But when you give someone something that you want, rather than what they need, you don't become more important in their eyes, you become a NetMinus. You waste their time, opportunities, and resources on unhelpful solutions. They figure this out after a few interactions with you, and they start turning to people who understand and meet their real needs.

If you offer them solutions that don't meet their real needs, you haven't seen it from their side, and you shouldn't be surprised if they turn to someone who "gets" their problem.

The key is listening, empathy, and "street smarts." We learn by listening, and then work to understand what we hear. When colleagues, clients, and connections are talking about their business needs, are you really paying attention? Are you really processing what they are saying? Or are you spending the time while they are speaking composing your response, or your proposal? Empathy means putting yourself into someone else's shoes. When they talk about their goals or challenges, do you have the capacity to see those things from their perspective? If you offer them solutions that don't meet their real needs, you haven't seen it from their side, and you shouldn't be surprised if they turn to someone who "gets" their problem.

"Street smarts" are practical pieces of knowledge based on experience. People who have been there, done that, and can show me how to get it done myself are NetPlus people on my balance sheet. The whole point of street smarts is that they cannot be taught, only learned "on the street" (through experience in the school of hard knocks). For example, when I travel to foreign countries that are very different from the United States, I like to use a local guide who can show me where the best places to eat or shop might be, and to help me negotiate in the marketplace for the best prices on gifts, supplies, or excursions. I can read travel guides or search the internet, but to know all the ins and outs of a strange city, you need someone who lives there, has developed street smarts, and can navigate all the subtle cultural differences. When it comes to working with someone back home on a project, especially if it's in an industry or network that I'm unfamiliar with, I want someone who has that kind of experiential wisdom. If that's not you, I'm sorry, but you aren't the help I need.

4. Do you solve problems? Or are you perplexed by them? Do you create them?

I need people around me who can solve my problems, but I also need people who I can give responsibility to without worrying. Can I trust you, and turn my attention elsewhere? Will you be able to handle the job I give you, manage the relationship with the connection I make for you, or follow through on the opportunity I give you? Will you be high maintenance? Will I have to watch over your shoulder, constantly helping you, or clean up your messes?

Some people are good at problem solving. Perhaps it's an innate ability, but whether it's a project in trouble, an unhappy client, a financial difficulty, a missed shipment, a crashed computer, lost data, a problem employee, or a canceled flight, NetPlus people take it in stride, find a solution, and move on. They tell me afterward that there was a problem, but that it has been solved and everything is back on track. People like that are NetPlus assets.

I need people around me who can solve my problems, but I also need people who I can give responsibility to without worrying. Can I trust you, and turn my attention elsewhere?

Are you flummoxed when things don't go according to plan? Do you over or under react, get angry, defensive, or depressed? Do you lash out or lay down? Do you know when to ask for help when you really need it, or do you call for rescue at the slightest adversity, or wait until it's too late?

Have you gone through your career stirring up problems where no problems existed before? Whenever judgment is called for, do you have a knack for doing the wrong thing? Be honest with yourself: are you someone who other people can trust to handle their opportunities and resources without worrying? That definitely influences whether they consider you a NetPlus or NetMinus.

5. Do you see yourself as a victim?

If you think of yourself as a victim, it may come from a sense of entitlement (see question number 1, above). But what paralyzes someone with a victim mentality is that they see themselves as a passive actor in their own story. In their understanding of their own life, things happen to them. They do not set agendas: they believe that others have controlled them. They do not initiate action, things are done to them. It's always someone else's fault.

Your victim mentality is a self-fulfilling prophecy: people avoid you, and if you can't be eliminated from an organization, you are always marginalized. This, of course, just confirms what you suspected all along, that everyone is out to get you.

When you think of the setbacks in your career, do you consider them to be the fault of those around you? Did the competitor lie, was the boss an idiot, was the company run by crooks, were the leads terrible, were your team members slackers and incompetents, were the computers old, were the rules unfair, did the dog eat your homework, etc.? As you tell your story, is it about others who were always villains or nincompoops, while you were tossed about like flotsam and jetsam in the tide? Were you always prevented from succeeding?

If so, you never will succeed, and every new connection you make will probably get tired of your whining. Ironically, your victim mentality is a self-fulfilling prophecy: people avoid you. If you can't be eliminated from an organization, you are always marginalized. This, of course, just confirms what you suspected all along, that everyone is out to get you.

There is almost no more certain way to become a NetMinus asset than to have a victim mentality. It is a worldview, and a terrible character defect. If it describes you, then you probably think that I'm picking on you right now. But I urge you, from the bottom of my heart to address this issue in your life. It may take counseling or a dramatic change in your character, but it is making you a NetMinus to almost everyone you work with.

6. Do you introduce or invite the NetPlus people around you to connect? Do you actively work to be a connector?

You may have a great network, but do you share it? Are you a gateway, a conduit for NetPlus people to meet each other? Or are you a gatekeeper, someone who holds onto your connections with a tight grip, forcing other people to always go through you? If so, that is controlling behavior, a power play to keep you necessary, and a strategy that usually backfires in the end. People may need you now, but they come to resent your control and ego in the process. You aren't genuinely a NetPlus to them, but a NetMinus that has to be tolerated for what you bring to the bargaining table. You may be able to run that game for a long time, but as soon as the people around you have a legitimate alternative—either by establishing their own, direct relationships within your network, or expanding their own through a NetPlus person—they will not need you anymore and drop you like a hot rock.

NetPlus people are always connecting the best people around them, enjoying the rising tide of energy that lifts everyone's boat.

A real NetPlus person wants to connect valuable professionals. It gives them pleasure, and they love to be part of a NetPlus community. They are always connecting the best people around them, enjoying the rising tide of energy that lifts everyone's boat. They not only pass on contact information, they go out of their way to make the introduction, and then stand back and watch the fun.

7. How are your people skills?

Almost all of us need to work with other people, whether colleagues, contractors, clients, or connections. And a huge part of our success depends on the quality of those relationships. You might have valuable knowledge and skills, but if you are difficult to work with, then you are a NetMinus that they cannot afford to do without—for the moment. Once they have an alternative, you will be quickly marginalized.

Remember how in grade school the teacher would evaluate how well you "played with others?" The skills learned on the playground last through life. Can you get along with others, even when you aren't alike or don't agree? Do people enjoy interacting with you, or dread it? Do they like you, or merely tolerate you? Are you the glue that holds teams together, or the wedge that drives them apart? Are clients eager to buy from you, or do they have to because of supply and price? Do you pick fights and start conflicts, or are you a peacemaker who brings everyone back to the table?

If you have built useful networks, everyone will like having you around, because through the strength of your contact list you are a walking Swiss Army knife.

---

8. Are your contacts useful?

NetPlus people make other people's world bigger by connecting them to useful people and organizations. If I need something that they can't provide, they know who can.

Are you connected to people and companies that are not only interesting, but of practical value? This is a sure-fire way to become a NetPlus person. NetPlus people know that they can't, and shouldn't even try, to be able to do everything well. Have you built networks of connections, and maintained those relationships, so that they can always find the right person or organization at the right time? If so, everyone will like having you around, because through the strength of your contact list you are a walking Swiss Army knife.

You may know a lot of people, and you may be willing to make connections and introductions for me, but will they be valuable? Will you make my world bigger and better by introducing me to NetPlus people who will make it even bigger and better? If not, then start intentionally building your network to be a toolbox of valuable resources.

9. Are you interested and invested in the wider world around you?

Earlier, I said that NetPlus people are like walking Swiss Army knives because of all the solutions and connections they carry with them. But NetMinus people are narrowly focused on their own interests and concerns. They go through life with tunnel vision, not looking around at things that don't immediately or directly affect them. As a result, they might be very knowledagble about a few things, but they are ignorant of other fields and have limited connections outside of their own industry. The NetPlus realizes that we can never really anticipate change, and is prepared to draw on their awareness of the wider world to react to new circumstances and opportunties.

10. Do you teach others what they need to know?

We have all heard the old expression, "Give a man a fish and he eats for a day; teach a man to fish and he eats for a lifetime." Along with solving other people's problems and introducing them to people who can solve the problems they can't, NetPlus people teach others to solve their own problems. They not only suggest solutions, they can show you how to implement them.

• • •

"People who fight fire with fire usually
end up with ashes."
— Abigail Van Buren

connections

chapter 4

Respect Other People's Balance Sheets

Shakespeare's plays are full of the pain—and folly—of unrequited love. One of the most painful experiences in life is to realize that someone else doesn't share the feelings you have for them.

Most of us remember what it was like to discover this for the first time, usually in school. Maybe you considered yourself part of a group of friends, but when it came time to form teams for some game, your "friends" didn't pick you. Maybe you had a crush on a boy or girl, daydreaming about going to a dance with them and wrote their name over and over on your notebook, only to be told that they wanted to "stay friends." Maybe you had a professor that you considered to be a special mentor, only to find out that some rival student was invited to the professor's house for dinner, or given a summer internship. Hopefully, by the time we grow up and begin our careers, we've learned enough from these relational debacles to head them off in adulthood, or at least how to cope with them when they do. Because, of course, we work with people everyday whose feelings for us don't match the ones we have for them.

One of the things we should have learned along the way is that other people are, well, other people. They have other backgrounds, other personalities and values, other needs and wants. They face other pressures and other agendas. They are not us. And when we project our perspective onto them, we aren't respecting their individuality, their "otherhood." Reducing other people to versions of ourself with different clothes is immature on our part, and disrespectful to them. It is also a foolish fantasy, which is bound to backfire and hurt us.

It pains me to see people who never really understand why they got fired, or lost a client. They might listen to their boss's words or the client's explanations, but they don't hear. They don't"get it."

Setting aside affairs of the heart and best-friend status, being unable to understand and respect other people's perception of us can wreak havoc in our professional relationships—which can deeply damage our career or business. It pains me to see people who never really understand why they got fired, or lost a client. They might listen to their boss's words or the client's explanations, but they don't hear. They don't "get it." Often, that's because they cannot overcome projecting their feelings onto the other person, and cannot grasp that things might look very different from the other person's vantage point.

If you have ever managed other people, then you know that the priorities of the people under you are often very different from your own. Time management systems often tell us to rank our tasks and problems; big, urgent problems are "A's," while things that can wait are "B's," or even "C's." Things that aren't worth your time are "D's." But the leader of an organization quickly realizes that people often come to him or her with problems that are "A problems" on their list, but are C's (or even D's) on the leader's list.

Often the leader will act sympathetically, nodding their head and appearing to care as much about the problem as the person for whom it is an A-priority. The follower walks out of the leader's office, believing that they were heard, and that the leader will take action. When the leader doesn't act on the issue, or distances him or herself from it, the follower is confused or even feels betrayed.

But the follower has made the mistake of not understanding that the leader is another person, with a different perspective on the organization, and has priorities that may not match theirs.

A painful truth, that all of us may have to swallow at some time, is that someone who is a NetPlus on our balance sheet might consider us to be a NetMinus on theirs.

What does this have to do with being a NetPlus person? I'm leading up to a painful truth, that all of us may have to swallow at some time: someone who is a NetPlus on our balance sheet might consider us to be a NetMinus on theirs. You may not be able to comprehend this, anymore than you could fathom unrequited love during your teenage years. This also may mean that you may be missing important cues and clues in your dealings with this person. If it is a coworker, you might misunderstand their actions in the workplace. If it is a client, you might overestimate their interest or commitment to your company. When they finally act to make it clear that they don't consider you a NetPlus—by passing you over for some other opportunity or buying from another supplier, or worse, firing you—you cannot comprehend how this could have happened. But I thought you liked me as much as I like you..., you think. It's like going to high school all over again.

The negative emotions then run wild. Shock, denial, anger, rationalization, and all the rest. You have to explain to others how you didn't get the assignment, blew the deal, or lost the client, or your job. The only thing worse than the feelings and the consequences is if you never understood what happened, because then you can't and won't learn anything from it. And if you don't learn anything, you are likely to repeat the same mistakes over and over again throughout your career.

So, here's a critical NetPlus tip: respect other people's relational balance sheets.

Take a look at the qualities of NetPlus and NetMinus people again, and consider the possibility that another person might have different needs, wants, and likes. For example, conversational topics that energize you might not energize someone else. You might be passionate about something: politics, religion, a hobby, a sports team, whatever. Maybe you love to travel for business. You take every opportunity to get on the road to see clients, or go to industry trade shows.

Anyone that gives you the opportunity for a business trip is a NetPlus person on your balance sheet. But have you considered that the colleague that accompanies you might hate to travel? Or that the client who has to meet you at an industry event dreads the trip? They see your invitations—which to you are opportunities to deepen the relationship—as irritating and useless wastes of their time. All of those trade shows with your boss or client dinners, which you thought were earning you the promotion or the deal, were draining your account with them. They start to decline to go on trips with you, or decline the invitation to dinner, and you panic.

Or, perhaps, you share information with them that you think is useful. But you don't understand their pressures and needs, and what is practical to you is irrelevant to them. The more that you send them information they can't use, the more you become a NetMinus on their balance sheet.

Obviously, the key is to understand other people by listening and observing with a healthy dose of empathy. But in order for that to be possible, you have to respect other people's right to be different, and to feel differently about you than you do about them. NetPlus people respect other people's individuality. NetMinus people narcissistically project their own personalities and priorities on everyone they meet. Which are you?

• • •

"In the business world, the rearview mirror is always clearer than the windshield."
— Warren Buffett

chapter 5

Do The Right Thing For The Right Reason

None of us like to be used, manipulated, or flattered.

OK, maybe we like to be flattered—a bit. Until it becomes patronizing or condescending. And it can be fun to be on the receiving end of a little manipulation, at least at the front end, when the manipulator is bribing us with favors. But the fun ends when the favors have to be returned. And most of us get angry when we realize that we are being used.

Too often, networking and sales involves using people. The process is obvious: discover the target's likes and dislikes, and uncover his or her values, needs, and wants. Then the slick networker talks about what interests the contact has, compliments the contact incessantly, does favors, offers hospitality and perks. It works, too, for the reasons in the last paragraph. And if the networker or salesman is any good, they know just how thick to lay it on and when to back off, so that the target doesn't get alienated and cut the connection.

You can use that approach, and you might be successful. In fact, you might be extraordinarily successful. Every week I meet people who have made a lot of money—or won high political office—by using flattery and manipulation to get what they want. It's a perfectly legitimate strategy.

People who use people often appear to be NetPlus, but it doesn't last long. Because a user and taker can only give so much, before they have to start taking. And when the flattery becomes condescending and the bill for the perks and favors comes due, the target moves the user into their NetMinus column.

But it's not what NetPlus is all about. People who use people often appear to be NetPlus, but it doesn't last long. Because a user and taker can only give so much, before they have to start taking. And when the flattery becomes condescending and the bill for the perks and favors comes due, the target moves the user into their NetMinus column. Every one of us has been a target of flattery and manipulation at one time or another, and most of us have tried it in our business life at least once. We tried to "work" someone to make a sale, or get a promotion, or get introduced to some important contact they knew. But eventually, our wick burned down and we used up all of our chips. The person we had worked over for that opportunity began to turn a cold shoulder to us. We couldn't understand it—after all: we thought we had a great relationship with them. What we didn't realize is that, in their relational accounting, we had begun to cost more than we were worth. They might have bought something, or made that introduction, because they felt obligated by what we had done for them. But then they realized that it was a quid pro quo. They paid their bill by buying our solution, or returning the favor, or passing on the contact. And then, they were done. Our calls and emails stopped being returned promptly. They didn't invite us to meet any more of their contacts.

Now, that might be OK with you. You got the sale, or the lead to obtain more sales. They weren't going to buy anything else from you anyway, right? You can deposit the check, count your money, and move on to your next target. And if that's all that matters to you, then there are a thousand books or workshops about networking and sales that you can read or use.

But that's not what it means to be a NetPlus person. NetPlus people aren't content with a quick, one time sale. They understand that business is a marathon, not a sprint. NetPlus people believe in the Golden Rule: do unto others as you would have others do unto you. They are genuine in their complements. They don't do favors only to obligate the other person to return the favor. They don't make introductions as a form of manipulation and quid pro quo.

NetPlus people are the same person when they are at work, volunteering for a charitable organization, talking to a neighbor across the fence, or standing in line at a busy coffee shop, waiting to place their order. They don't have to shift from one mode of behavior to another.

Some of you might be thinking,"That sounds great, but I'm in business to make a profit, for my employer and myself. I have a boss to account to, and a family to provide for. Being a do-gooder to everyone I meet might be noble, but it doesn't pay my employees or my bills."

Don't get me wrong. There is a place for non-profit activities. Volunteer for a charitable organization, etc. But we are all in business to make a net profit. I wrote this book because I genuinely want to help people succeed, but I also want to make money selling copies of it.

But here's the thing: NetPlus people are the same person when they are at work, volunteering for a charitable organization, talking to a neighbor across the fence, or standing in line at a busy coffee shop waiting to place their order. They don't have to shift from one mode of behavior to another. Look again at the list of NetPlus qualities. NetPlus isn't something they just do at work: it's baked into their character. It's who they are.

NetPlus people go through their career treating others fairly and justly, not as a means to an end, but as an end in itself. They believe that if they are generous and gracious and useful, that they will create a generous and gracious and useful world around them.

NetPlus people go through their career treating others fairly and justly, not means to an end, but as an end in itself. They believe that if they are generous and gracious and useful, that they will create a generous and gracious and useful world around them.

And that's where the profit comes from. As they move through life and their career, they create a wake behind them, like a boat. If you've ever driven a ski boat on a small lake, like we have here in Michigan, you know that your wake hits the shore and bounces back. Not only that, but all the other boats on the lake that are weaving around each other, towing wake boards and skiers, are also kicking up a wake. All the waves intersect and ricochet off each other, until the lake is full of chop. Applied to business, if we create wakes of generosity and graciousness and fairness behind us, and if those around us do the same, we will receive back, ten or one hundred fold, what we invested into our community. To use another nautical metaphor, the rising tide will lift all the boats.

The opposite is also true. We could go through our careers creating wakes of using, taking, and manipulation. People may buy from us, and we may be able to afford the nicest boat on our local lake, but we will be known as NetMinus people. This will then create a NetMinus culture in our company, community, or marketplace. What we create will come back around and slap into our bow like a nasty chop. It may even capsize us when we least expect it.

• • •

"Be civil to all; sociable to many; familiar with few; friend to one; enemy to none."
— Benjamin Franklin

chapter 6

Dealing with NetMinus People

What do you do with the NetMinus people in your professional life? Before I answer that, let me stress that I'm talking about your professional life. We all have personal relationships with people that take more than they give, which we cannot and *should not* avoid. At times, children, aged parents, siblings or other extended family members might all take more from you than they give back, making your world smaller and worse. I believe that our family bonds are sacred; the Ten Commandments tell us to honor our father and mother, for example. We should be good and generous neighbors, even if we live next door to a difficult person. I also believe that each of us should be giving of our time and resources and gifts to charity, to help others who can't help us in return.

Our family bonds are sacred, we should be good and generous neighbors, and we should be giving of our time and resources to charity. But when it comes to our business lives, our opportunities and resources are limited. We have an obligation to the people who depend on us to spend our opportunities and resources wisely.

But when it comes to our business lives, our opportunities and resources are limited. If I spend an hour with someone, or take them along to meet one of my contacts, I can't have that hour or connection opportunity back to spend it on someone else. It is an opportunity cost. And I have an obligation to the people who depend on me (my employer, my employees, my investors, my family, the charities I donate to, etc.) to spend my opportunities and resources where they will give the biggest return possible. This means that in my professional life I need to identify the NetMinus people and minimize my investment in them. If I schedule a lunch with a NetMinus contact, or connect them with an opportunity, I'm working to put limits on my professional world.

Dealing With NetMinus People

You can't eliminate all of the NetMinus people in your organization or professional networks. Not everyone can be above average. There is a bell-curve of attributes, and some people are more interesting, or more knowledgeable, or better-connected, than others. Also, and it is crucial that you remember this, someone who is NetPlus on your balance sheet might be NetMinus on someone else's. They might be a valuable asset to someone else in your organization, or in your network. They might not be worth your time or investment, but eliminating them altogether might do more harm than good if it negatively impacts someone else that is valuable to you.

So, what do you do with the NetMinus people in your professional world? Let's take a moment and review the qualities of a NetMinus person:

1. *Take More Than They Give in Relationships*

2. *Make Me Feel Tired, Depressed, Angry, or Frightened*

3. *Give Me What They Want to Give, Not What I Need*

4. *Create Problems Wherever They Go*

5. *See Themselves as Victims*

6. *Don't Make Connections for Me At All, Or If They Do, It Is To Other NetMinus People*

7. *Shrink My Contact List*

8. *Not Interested In Anything Outside Of Their Own Narrow Field Of Self-Interest*

9. *Don't Know Where To Find Solutions, Ideas, or Opportunities*

10. *Give me information, but not useful knowledge*

If you think about it, the first five items are character-personality traits, which are hard to change. It's very difficult to train someone to become a different sort of person. When you realize that half of the things that make a person a NetMinus to you are inherent in their basic character and personality, the answer to the question, "What do I do with the NetMinus people in my professional life?" begins to take shape: this is who they are, and you can't easily fix them. You may not be able to eliminate them from your schedule, but you must limit them on your calendar and within your contacts.

The last five items are learnable skills. You can teach someone to be a better problem-solver or networker, or the value of doing research and offering solutions. I believe in the power of modeling: people are social creatures, and will usually adapt themselves to the behavior of the leader or the culture of the group. You can make positive use of the peer-pressure dynamic by spending time showing them how to do it. Even something as simple as taking them along to a meeting, or letting them watch how you interact with new contacts, is modeling a new standard. If they are observant, adaptable, and (most of all) teachable, they can move the last five items on the above list into the NetPlus column. That might be enough to make them NetPlus overall, if their personality and character issues don't spoil their performance.

The first five qualities of a NetMinus person are character-personality traits, which are hard to change. It's very difficult to train someone to become a different sort of person.

A Contradiction?

Some of you are thinking, "If NetPlus people make everyone else's world bigger and better, then why would they not invest in the NetMinus people around them?" The confusion is understandable. After all, withholding time and opportunities is not making the NetMinus person's world bigger and better. Some readers are thinking, *Ken, it sounds like you are contradicting yourself when you say we should invest in them based whether we will get a return on our investment.*

Of course we observe differences between people's performance and ability. It would be irresponsible not to, especially if we supervise them. And it would be unfair to reward people based on something other than their performance (or potential performance).

Let me clarify. The premise of this book is that we all have a relational balance sheet, on which we inevitably (though often unconsciously) rank our professional relationships based on whether they are a bottom line asset to us. No one should apologize for this, it is simply acknowledging the reality that we learn more from some people than others. For example: some employees sell more than others, some people produce more work in a day than others, some solve problems more quickly and require less assistance. Of course we observe these differences, it would be irresponsible not to, especially if we supervise them. And it would be unfair to reward people based on something other than their performance (or potential performance).

A NetPlus person understands that if they are not delivering value to someone else, that person has a responsibility to invest their time elsewhere. The NetPlus person who realizes that they are a NetMinus on someone else's sheet either accepts that, or works to change so that they are providing value.

A NetPlus person does try to make everyone else's world bigger and better, even the people who are NetMinuses to him, just because it's the right thing to do. A NetPlus person never has ill will towards the NetMinus people on his balance sheet and will not unjustly harm their business or career. A NetPlus person does everything possible for those who cost more than they deliver. But a NetPlus person also respects other people's balance sheets. A NetPlus person understands that if they are not delivering value to someone else, that person has a responsibility to invest their time elsewhere. The NetPlus person who realizes that they are a NetMinus on someone else's sheet either accepts that, or works to change it so that they are providing value. I don't expect the governor of my state to take my calls or accept my invitation to show up at my local charity golf outing, because I can't provide enough value to be worth his time. On the other hand, if I realize that my boss didn't take me with him to the conference because I don't know enough about the subject matter, I study and work harder before next conference.

I can only have five (or less) lunch meetings a week. I can only travel to so many events, and I can't afford to take everyone who wants to go with me. My budget only lets me hire or promote a finite number of people. It would be unwise and unfair to invest in people based on something other than merit and performance (or a smart bet on potential performance).

So, while a NetPlus person tries to make a bigger and better world for even the NetMinus people on his list, he has to balance this against his responsibility to use his time, opportunities, and resources well. I can only have five (or less) lunch meetings a week. I can only travel to so many events, and I can't afford to take everyone who wants to go with me.

My budget only lets me hire or promote a finite number of people. I do everything I can for the NetMinus people on my list, but it would be unwise and unfair to invest in people based on something other than merit and performance (or a smart bet on potential performance), relevant to my responsibilities.

Difficult Conversations

Spending less opportunities and resources on NetMinus people will inevitably lead to some difficult conversations. A NetMinus will notice that you passed on meeting with them, and took someone else to lunch, or that you don't often call on them to speak in meetings, or passed over them for a project, or that you didn't take them to meet a valuable potential client. And they will want to know why.

Usually, this manifests itself as awkwardness. Most people are not direct enough to come right out and ask you why, but there is tension in the relationship. The easy thing to do (which most of us choose) is to ignore it. When we are with the NetMinus person, we keep the conversation focused on anything except why we are investing less in them. But is that the right thing to do? Shouldn't a NetPlus person try and help the NetMinus to improve? Do we owe them an explanation for our actions?

> *The biggest challenge for most Net-Minus people is that they rarely realize that they are NetMinus, and if they do, they almost never figure out why. They never "get it." This lack of self-understanding can cripple their career.*

The biggest challenge for most NetMinus people is that they rarely realize that they are NetMinus, and if they do, they almost never figure out why. They never "get it." This lack of self-understanding can cripple their career. When they lose a job or a deal, or are left on the sidelines when assignments are given out or professionals are connecting at an event, they blame their lack of success on all sorts of things. People with victim mindsets can always identify something they believe is thwarting their efforts. Sometimes, they get caught into a loop of shame and self-loathing which only compounds their problems. What they need to do is remove their ego from the situation, and be as objective as possible. They need to grasp that they didn't make a bigger or better world for the person who considered them a NetMinus. They might be a NetPlus for other people, and if so, then they need to invest more of themselves with people that consider them an asset. But if there is a pattern developing in their career—they are consistently being considered NetMinuses—then they may need to make some important changes.

Should you help them evalute themselves and make changes? This would inevitably involve a difficult conversation. No one wants to hear bad news about himself or herself, and none of us want to be the bearer of that news. Before I talk to a NetMinus person about why they are NetMinus and how it is hurting their career, I ask myself five questions.

1. **Do I really understand their problem?** I may think that I understand why they are NetMinus, or how that might be holding back their career. But I may not have enough information to really make that judgment. I might only know them in one context, and there might be more to the story. For example, I've played in golf leagues with men who get incredibly angry and vulgar on the golf course. They are not much fun to be around, and some occasionally complain about how their careers are not advancing as they would like. I'm tempted to tell them that they are not much fun to be around, and that based on our time together I certainly wouldn't want to hire or work with them. But I check myself, because the only context I know them in is a recreational setting for a few hours a week. Perhaps there is more to them, or their story, than I see. We should always make sure we have enough facts before sharing an opinion, especially if it might hurt someone.

2. **Do I have the position or permission to tell them the truth?** Everyday I meet someone whose behavior leads me to assume that they are most likely a NetMinus person. But it's not always my place to share my observations with them. They might be new acquaintances, or not especially close connections. Or they might be the employee or family member of an colleague. I'm not in a position to give them advice or even correction. That needs to come from their family member, or their boss, or colleagues. They also might not want to hear my input. We all need to give and get permission to be able to have difficult conversations. Sometimes that's explicit (we ask for someone's input), and sometimes it's implied (a boss has a right, or even an obligation, to correct an employee that is out of line, whether the subordinate wants to hear it or not). Before I give critical advice to a NetMinus person, I want to be sure that I'm really the right person to be doing so.

3. **Are they capable of hearing me?** As I said earlier, one of the problems with NetMinus people is that they often don't realize that they are NetMinus. They don't "get it." If someone's ego, state of mind, or emotions prevent them from being able to understand and process constructive criticism will accomplish very little. The ability to see yourself as others see you and to hear their suggestions for improvement requires maturity, emotional security, and a receptiveness to change.

A difficult conversation with someone who lacks these qualities, or someone who otherwise does but is suffering from some stress or trauma at the time, is insensitive and pointless. The exception to this rule is if I have an obligation, as a boss or team leader, to make someone accountable for their actions by giving them an evaluation, even if it will be painful for them to hear.

4. **Am I willing to risk their reaction?** Difficult conversations have unpredictable outcomes, but they can lead to negative reactions. The other person could become angry, despondent, or vindictive. They could become violent, or do something to harm themselves, sever the relationship, or seek revenge by damaging our business or reputation. Sometimes, the possibility of helping the person improve is worth taking the risk, but sometimes it is not. If I'm not willing to accept the possible consequences, it's best to wait until a better opportunity to share comes along (if it ever does).

5. **Can I truly do it for their benefit?** We know that criticism should be constructive, but sometimes we are tempted to share a critique out of our own frustration or insecurity. We might tell ourselves that our comments are for their own good, but we may really be indulging our own need to feel superior, or even to hurt them for something they have done to us. If I can't be

genuine in my attempt to offer helpful critique, it's best to wait until I can.

Writing this chapter has been difficult for me; this is an unpleasant topic. I naturally prefer to believe in and trust people. Most are honest, genuine, and really want to be helpful. But it's very difficult when we find ourselves having to work with or for those who are not.

I teach my children to not worry or stress about situations that are out of their control, to take them head on and learn from them. I want them to stay positive and look for the paths in front of them that will lead to the best possible results. If you are working with or for a NetMinus person, or if you suspect that you might be a NetMinus to many of the people around you, it's not too late to change for the better. You can't undo what is behind you. But you can begin today to improve your own world by resolving to make everyone else's world bigger and better.

• • •

"As I grow older, I pay less attention to what men say.
I just watch what they do."
—Andrew Carnegie

Part II
Make Their World Bigger and Better

Chapter 7

Be a Gateway,
Not a Gatekeeper
(A Connector, Not a Controller)

The world is bigger than we are.

That seems obvious, doesn't it? But, while we may agree with that statement, many of us don't act as if it's true. Some of us obsess so much about our own small circle of connections that we come to believe that business is like a pie: it's all about who gets how much of a finite resource. How much of the money, time, or attention in your circle of connections will go to you and how much will go to your competitor?

People who grow successful businesses don't think that way, because they know that the world is bigger than just their world. And because they know that, they are not forced to divide the existing pie. They make the pie bigger, or bake more pies, or find other people who are making pies.

So, in case you get overly focused on your set of connections, remember this: there are more people than you've met, more industries than the one you work in, more knowledge than you understand, and—most importantly, if you want to grow your business—far more opportunities than you know about.

The question you should be asking is, "How do I get connected to the bigger world that's around me?" I have two answers to that question. First, build relationships with NetPlus people, because they will make your world bigger. Second, be a NetPlus person, and make everyone else's world bigger by introducing them to people, organizations, industries, knowledge, and opportunities that they don't already know about.

I love the giant Gateway Arch in Saint Louis. It commemorates the possibilities, and risks, that generations of pioneers took in moving west of the Mississippi. I also like how large it is, because it reminds me that I should be a wide and generous gateway, freely sharing who and what I know.

NetPlus people are gateways to the bigger world around us. As we have seen, two of the qualities of a NetPlus person are that they have connections to other NetPlus people, and they are knowledgeable of and plugged into the larger world. They introduce us to individuals, places, solutions, and ideas that help us to discover opportunities that were always there, but that we didn't know about because we were focused with tunnel vision on our own set of people and problems.

I work hard to stay aware of any opportunities that crop up around me, so that I can be a gateway for friends, co-workers, business associates, my children, and their friends. College students need the most help these days connecting to the right opportunity that could help them for their future. Recently, my son's friend Annie was visiting our house. She was concerned because she was studying to be a dental hygienist, but had a personal connection with only one dentist. That dentist's office was in a very, very small town south of Grand Rapids. They weren't hiring and there was no possibility of any kind of internship. I asked her if I could help. She agreed, and so I shared my connections in the dental business: two former classmates, and my current dentist. I also know two orthodontists, one of which is close to my family. You could almost hear her say, "BINGO!" behind her excited eyes. Later, she told my son Jake that she is so happy to be his friend and is now looking forward to pursuing these opportunities in her life. If you have teenagers or young adults in your house, spend time going out to dinner with them and their friends. Find out what they aspire to do, and then help them make connections within your network. Your children will appreciate you and their friends will respect you for investing in their future. One day, that connection you make for them might turn around and open an opportunity for you.

People who grow successful businesses don't think about carving the pie, because they know that the world is bigger than than just their world. And because they know that, they are not forced to divide the existing pie. They make the pie bigger, or bake more pies, or find other people who are making pies.

Everyday, I try to be that sort of gateway in all aspects of my life. I do my best to enlarge the opportunities of the people I meet by making connections for them. In order to do that, I have to understand exactly what they want. If I don't understand their goals and needs, I can't make a perfect match for them with another connection. As I try to match connections to their needs, I've noticed at least two things that can limit my ability to share the wider world with them. First, I can't share what I don't know. I have to be constantly learning, making new connections, and adding to my contact list. That means getting their contact info. It doesn't do any good for me to tell someone that I "know a guy" who can help them, if I don't know how to reach that guy. Adding them to my contact list is critical. There are lots of great tools out there for that (smart phones, social media applications, old fashioned business cards and address books, etc.). The important thing is that I have some way of cataloguing connections so that I can easily make connections between my connections.

Second, I have to let go of my need to be in control. It feels good to tell someone that I know a person or organization that can help them, and then be the power broker in the introduction. It makes me look important to two of my connections. It forces people who want increased opportunities to go through me, and to make them acknowledge and thank me. It puts them in my debt, making them owe me a favor. It lets me pick winners and losers, and feel powerful by rewarding my friends and punishing my enemies. These are all normal human motives, but they are the worst side of our nature. They come from insecurity and naked ambition, greed and vindictiveness. In most instances, they are petty: most of us aren't talking about getting a private audience with the president or the pope. We are simply being control freaks and lusting for power over others for its own sake.

If I give in to those motives, I'm no longer a gateway, I'm a gatekeeper. We've all met gatekeepers. Any of us who have worked in sales are far too familiar with the contact in an organization who forces all communication to go through them. They will say that they are protecting the time of others, but often it's really just a naked power play. But I have to admit that, at times, I have fallen into behaving like a gatekeeper myself. I have known people, or businesses, that could both benefit by getting to know each other. It would have been fairly easy for me to make those connections. And yet, sometimes I hesitated. Why?

Sometimes, we become control freaks, lusting for power over others for its own sake. If I give into those motives, I'm no longer a gateway, I'm a gatekeeper.

Sometimes, I hesitate to make connections between people because the timing might be wrong. I know that they both have something the other needs, but perhaps one of them is not ready for the introduction. Maybe their product or service is not available at this time—they might be overwhelmed with demand, or improving something to bring to market, or just too busy at the moment. I certainly don't want to make an introduction, much less set up a meeting for someone, if the other party isn't going to be able to give their attention to the new connection. If I do, I squander the opportunity for both parties to develop the relationship.

For example, I met a young man working as a valet in front of one of my favorite restaurants. John owned the valet service and had several employees working with him. John was an innovator, and when I had a few minutes to chat he would share his ideas with me. Not every idea needed my help for a connection but I did listen, and over time I became friends with John. One recent evening, John shared with me an idea that he had been working on. He was excited, but wasn't sure what his next step should be. His idea sparked my interest enough to invite him over to my home that evening to meet with a few of my NetPlus friends for a friendly game of cards. Later in the evening while we were playing, he brought up his idea and one of my friends seemed very intrigued with the concept. He was impressed enough to offer a meeting with an "angel investor" that looks for new business concepts to invest in. It was exciting to watch this connection develop in front of my eyes. At the end of the evening, John stayed behind and we brainstormed some more about the next steps. After learning more, I knew it was too early for him to meet the angel lead. So I arranged a lunch meeting with two strong engineers (both of them NetPlus people) that were independent electronics consultants who did this kind of work and had years of industry experience. The lunch went well. John learned a lot about invention and the ideas the engineers shared were helpful, honest, and worth much more than the cost of the lunch. They are true NetPlus people and I'm glad to call them my friends.

There are other justifiable reasons for hesitating to make a connection. One of the parties might have asked you to keep your relationship with them quiet, and confidential. Maybe one of your connections is highly visible with a demanding position, who expects you to respect their limited time by not bringing too many new connections to them. Or perhaps you are suspicious of the motives of one of the parties. Helping to connect one of your friend's competitors to his best customer might be disloyal. Your job or business might involve making these sorts of relationships, and you need to secure some agreements first. And, of course, you would not introduce a severely NetMinus person to someone if you suspect that they will drain and abuse the new relationship.

However, our default position should be to be gateways, and not gatekeepers. NetPlus people are never motivated by petty control and power games.

• • •

You can make more friends in two months by be-coming really interested in other people than you can in two years by trying to get other people inter-ested in you. Which is just another way of saying that the way to make a friend is to be one.
— Dale Carnegie

Chapter 8

Be An Exponential Connection

Archimedes said, "Give me a long enough lever, and I can lift the world." Introduce me to the right people, and I can connect the world.

NetPlus people are gateways: they connect their contacts, and make everyone else's world bigger. But a real NetPlus person doesn't just introduce one person to another, they make exponential connections. Because they are aware of and savvy about the world, they know who and where the levers are, and how to work with them to lift the world.

NetPlus people are levers, who con-
tribute to the process of exponen-
tially connecting people, organiza-
tions, and ideas with the wider
world. They don't just know people,
they know and influence the right
people, who know and influence oth-
ers. A NetPlus person doesn't just en-
large your world one connection at a
time. They enlarge your world by
plugging you into people who are
plugged in themselves.

In Malcolm Gladwell's outstanding book, *The Tipping Point: How Little Things Can Make a Big Difference* (Little Brown, 2000), we learn about three kinds of people who are "levers," because their efforts and influence extends exponentially outward.

Connectors are the people who link others to the wider world. They have an extraordinary capacity to meet, connect, and maintain relationships with a large number of people. While these relationships are not always intimate, connectors are gifted acquaintances. While the average person can maintain about twenty or thirty friendships, Gladwell says that connectors have social networks of a hundred or more. While most of us focus on the quality of our relationships, connectors happily excel at quantity. Their connections are spread throughout multiple communities and industries. They are curious, self-confident, social, and energetic. They connect quickly, easily, and effortlessly, and can remember all the people that they meet. While some of us struggle to remember the names of people we run into on a fairly regular basis (the lady in the corner cubicle near the second floor elevator, or the guy we've met at a church function a half-dozen times), connectors have no such trouble. They go through life collecting contacts, and their networks spread far beyond what most of us can see or imagine.

Mavens are highly knowledgeable, eager and willing to share their knowledge to help others. As connectors collect contacts, mavens collect information. While they may not know as many people as the connectors, what they know is valuable and sought after. When they speak, people listen. And because mavens have a NetPlus character and lifestyle, they aren't the kind of people who would hold that information close to their chests or use it to extract favors from others. They genuinely want to help others learn and solve problems. So they speak often, whenever asked.

Salesmen are the third type of "lever" that Gladwell describes. They have a unique ability to influence others through persuasion and charisma. But they are not merely persuasive and charismatic; they are also powerful negotiators who understand how those around them think, and how to craft solutions that meet their needs.

Gladwell builds a case that "viral" ideas need all three types of "lever" people to spread through society like an epidemic. Mavens generate ideas, or develop the content of messages. Salesmen present ideas in an attractive context. And connectors provide the pathways that ideas travel along to reach other communities and markets. Along the way, new mavens, salesmen, and connectors pick up the messages and repeat the process, multiplying the effect exponentially.

In business, you hear all the time how important it is to know and understand your weaknesses. To admit you have a weakness is a gift to yourself because you now can grow and find the best connection to help you solve your weakness. I have a weakness. In fact, I have a few weaknesses. One of them is the ability to be a strong negotiator in the process of trying to "win" an argument or close an opportunity. I know this about myself, and it has cost me thousands of dollars over time in situations where I pushed too hard and people pulled back. The good news is that I know someone that is an incredible negotiator and still believes in my philosophy of NetPlus. His name is Mike Borowka, my Director of Business Development. He has done such a great job leading the sales team and creating "good" opportunities with our prospects that I recently named him President of Quantum Leap Communications. He has worked with me for over six years and has many gifts to offer the team, his family, and the community. You see, Mike is a NetPlus person and we are lucky to have to him in our organization. He understands his role in the business. As a maven and salesmen, he complements my role as the connector. It has become the perfect combination for our success.

NetPlus people are not all alike; they might be connectors, mavens, or salesmen. But what NetPlus people do have in common is that they are all levers, who contribute to the process of exponentially connecting people, organizations, and ideas with the wider world. They don't just know people, they know and influence the right people, who know and influence others. A NetPlus person doesn't just enlarge your world, one connection at a time. They enlarge your world by plugging you into people who are plugged in.

Are you a lever for your professional contacts? Do you make their world bigger one introduction at a time, or do you plug them into the wider world through connectors, mavens, and salesmen? Can you help them hopscotch their way to anywhere and anyone they need to know?

In the 1930s, people began discussing the notion that every person on earth might be linked by no more than "six degrees of separation" to every other person. List everyone you know or have come into contact with (classmates, coworkers, neighbors, etc.), and then list out the connections of everyone on your list. If all of these connections were mapped, with a network diagram, it would look like a vast roadmap, with hubs (people) connecting to hubs (other people) which branched even further out. The six degrees theory claims that everyone in the world is linked to everyone else in the world through no more than six connections on this map. Someone you know knows someone, who knows someone, who knows someone, who knows someone, who knows someone, who knows the prime minister of Norway or the factory worker who assembled my cell phone. Since the 1930's, social scientists and statisticians have debated this idea, and while they differ on whether the gap is really five degrees or seven, they agree that the point is valid: there are only a relatively small number of connections separating us and the rest of the world. NetPlus people are the levers that can help us move the world, because they are superconductors connecting people and ideas.

We have another Mike working for us at Quantum Leap. Mike Storrer has the gift of making exponential connections. He sought us out after the previous company he worked for went out of business during the recession of 2009. He heard about our NetPlus approach, and knew that he would thrive in our environment. Because he is such a NetPlus person, Mike rarely loses a client, and his connections enthusiastically tell others about how much they have enjoyed working with him. We often receive complimentary testimonials from customers about the value he has brought them. As NetPlus person working in a NetPlus company, over the last two years Mike has more than tripled his sales in comparison of all previous companies he's worked for in the past, exceeding even his expectations and being a part of the President's Club at Quantum Leap. He understands the value of exponential connections and the rewards that follow.

Are you a lever for your professional contacts? Do you make their world bigger one introduction at a time, or do you plug them into the wider world through connectors, mavens, and salesmen? Can you help them hopscotch their way to anywhere and anyone they need to know?

If you'd like to be that type of NetPlus person, there are a few practical steps you can take.

Identify the connectors, mavens, and salesmen that you know. They are the ones who can introduce you to the rest of the world, and your contacts as well. Learn everything you can from these people, and then emulate them by passing it on. Follow their example to become one of them.

Learn what interests the particular connectors, mavens, and salesmen that you know. They are individuals, not just "types." They don't exist to connect you or anyone else for no reason. They have backgrounds, needs, and personalities of their own. Figure out what would intrigue them, what would solve their problems. If you bring them people, ideas, or solutions that get their attention, you have the opportunity to get the attention of a vast sea of people and organizations that lie beyond them.

Always be introducing these levers to your NetPlus connections, and vice versa. You cannot predict where these connections might lead, but if you plug everyone around you into the world, you will be plugged in yourself. You and your professional contacts will be exposed to all sorts of opportunities and possibilities.

• • •

"How wonderful it is that nobody need wait a single moment before starting to improve the world."
— Anne Frank

Chapter 9

Put Skin in the Game

I started this book by saying that Facebook friends are not really friends, Twitter followers are not really followers, and you aren't really connected to anyone through LinkedIn.

This should be so obvious that I hate to point it out. Social media technologies (those are the most popular at this time, and I use all of them myself, but newer ones are sure to come along) are great tools to track and manage relationships, but they are not themselves business relationships. We need to be reminded of this, because these tools tempt us to believe that there are shortcuts to building relationships based on mutual interest and trust. There are, of course, anonymous business transactions: I buy gas everyday from a self-serve pump, or purchase something online through the Web. But those are just transactions, not relationships. I don't have any connections with the oil company that owns the gas station, or with the e-commerce company that sold and shipped the Christmas gift I just bought.

For the NetPlus person who wants to make everyone else's world bigger, social media technologies can have some value. We can help a colleague by posting a link to his website, or retweeting some news about her, or recommending their product or service to our contacts. But while doing so can be a real help, and is generous, it doesn't invest much of you in the connection. Of course, you did lend some of your credibility and visibility with that sort of a link but there isn't much of a relational investment.

For NetPluses, connecting others is natural, and part of their normal, daily activities. They might make a call, send a text, or dash off an email, but they think nothing of making a warm introduction within the context of their normal engagement with their network.

Relational investments are the most important type of business equity. While money would be the most obviously important form of equity in business, relationships might be a close second, if not the first. Think about it: hiring, investment, partnerships, collaboration, negotiating terms of a deal—all of these and more depend on relationships. How much money you can raise to start a business depends not only on the strength of your idea and business plan, but on how wide and deep your connections run in the business world. The right relationships can open doors, and can close them to competitors. Purchasing is not always a purely financial decision; loyalty, trust, and friendship often trump an extra dollar or two.

This is why we cannot afford to just post links, or hand out contact information, without putting some skin in the game. That means risking something of your own credibility and relational good will to help connect two of your connections. If you really believe that person A could be a benefit to person B, don't just give A's email or phone number to B and leave the interaction by chance. Call B yourself, and make a proactive ("warm") introduction. Or set up a meeting between the three of you, where you can facilitate the connection.

This may sound like a lot of work, and some of you are rolling your eyes right now. *Ken,* you're thinking, *you have no idea how busy I am. I don't have time to hand-hold every contact I pass along.* Well, I do know how busy you are. We all are. But just as great athletes make the extraordinary look effortless, NetPlus people make these sort of connections look easy.

NetPlus people are engaged with others, both inside and outside of their field. They may not all be extroverts, and they may have demanding schedules, but they constantly meet and develop relationships with other NetPluses. They have great people skills, and are often the social glue in relationships. It's not something that they have to make a conscious effort to do, because it flows out of their character and lifestyle. They communicate effectively and effortlessly. Connecting others is a natural part of their normal, daily activities. They might make a call, send a text, or dash off an email, but they think nothing of making a warm introduction within the context of their normal engagement with their network.

How do you put this in practice? You begin by thinking like a connector and a communicator. Almost every business interaction is an opportunity to share information, and to make introductions. Remember that introductory conversations don't need to be long, or deep. Sometimes, just a few sentences, a short email, or even a text message is enough for you to endorse a connection and make a warm introduction. When a NetPlus person shares a few words endorsing someone, even in a casual setting, it's enough for me to give the person serious consideration.

My cousin Andrew Padilla and his friend Jeremiah started a business called the Great American Culture

Company. They won a contest in Grand Rapids for the best new business idea. Their business model is a service to help Chinese students going to college in the United States get more quickly acclimated to American culture. Grand Valley State University has given them a classroom to use for teaching and "culturizing" the new Chinese students into our society. They go out shopping, bowling, to local restaurants, and even parties with these students, helping them to participate and have fun in a new country. The organizations in China that sponsor these students would pay a fee for this sort of cultural transition service.

I am privileged to be able to mentor and connect my cousin and his friend to relevant individuals and businesses that can benefit from their service. I have at least two college connections already in process with them along with three corporations, one of which is in China. Recently, they were both in China meeting with over fifty college placement offices. Jeremiah and Andrew are looking for students coming to the USA, specifically to Grand Rapids. These placement offices are the key the connection. I recommended that they throw a big party and invite all the sales staff from each office to eat, drink, and get to know Jeremiah and Andrew. In China, culture is about the relationship first, then business. A party was a great way to make an impression and win their trust. I can't wait to see how this web of connections between industry and academia in two countries will create opportunities over time that none of us anticipated.

If someone is worth recommending, then you should be investing relational equity and adding value into those introductions. You are cementing relationships between you and them based on mutual interest, shared experiences, and trust. You never know when, where, or how those relationships will pay dividends to everyone involved.

NetPlus people   also connect people at events with natural grace. If a NetPlus is in a room full of people, particularly a room full of interesting NetPluses, they are connecting. Their style might be deliberate and overt, or it might be more subtle and easygoing, but they want to meet others and learn from them. And when they do, they don't have to go out of their way to connect others. In fact, they don't have to remember to do it at all. It comes as second nature: if they meet someone who ought to know someone else, they make the introduction. It's not a chore for them; they genuinely want to see their contacts meet each other and make everyone's world get bigger and better. As I've said before, NetPluses know that a rising tide lifts all the boats, including theirs.

Do you put skin in the game when you connect your connections? Of course you want to be a gateway and not a gatekeeper. But simply sharing a link, or passing on an email, is a lazy and disengaged way to bring people together. You may be a gate, but you are nothing more than portal people pass through. To be a NetPlus person means being *engaged* in the process of bringing real people together. If someone is worth recommending, or two people should be introduced, then you should be investing relational equity and adding value into those introductions. If you do, then you are not only helping your contacts get to know each other, you are cementing the relationships between you and them based on mutual interest, shared experiences, and trust. You never know when, where, and how those relationships will pay dividends to everyone involved. But as I pointed out earlier in this chapter, these relationships are the real currency of professional world. Make everyone else's world bigger and better, and your world will become bigger and better as well.

• • •

"Act as if what you do makes a difference. It does."
— William James

Chapter 10

Networking Nightmares

Some people who hear about NetPlus from a third party assume that it is a business networking system. If you've gotten this far in the book, you know that it's not. Networking systems are fine, but we overemphasize their importance to business success. Networking is a powerful tool, but like most power tools, if used incorrectly it can cause injury. Poor networking can set your career back two steps for every step it takes you forward. Over the years, I've seen some real networking nightmares. To illustrate some of these mistakes, let me tell you a story.

Once upon a time there was a guy named Ned. He wanted his business to grow, in fact, he *needed* it to grow, as fast as possible. So Ned began to attend a local networking event.

The event was organized by a professional group whose purpose was to encourage local business professionals to mix and create opportunities for one another. It met once a month in a rented ballroom of hotel, and began with an hour of unstructured social time around the cash bar. Members would arrive, write their names on sticky name tags with a felt marker, grab a drink, and mingle. Eventually, the organizers would sit everyone down, there would be some announcements and introductions, and a guest speaker would make a presentation about a generic business topic. Afterward, members would continue mixing for another hour or so. It was like thousands of other such groups around the country.

Ned worked hard to get his money's worth out of the event. Unfortunately, Ned didn't make as many connections as he hoped.

Even though it was not a competition and there was no prize, Ned was determined to "win" the networking group. He wanted to be—and to be known as—the best networker there, and to make the most money by capturing more business at the event than anyone else. Ned was excited about his company, NedCo, and all the interesting "solutions" they offered, and he wanted to sell more of them. And so he came loaded for bear, with a giant stack of his business cards, and not one, but two kinds of brochures: trifold *and* full size!

Ned worked hard to get his money's worth out of the event. He shook as many hands as he could. He gave his elevator speech over and over. He shoved cards and brochures at anyone who was polite enough to listen to him. If anyone hesitated after this barrage, he moved in for the kill: smart phone in hand, calendar app open, he asked them what day next week they were free for lunch.

Unfortunately, Ned didn't make as many connections as he hoped at the event because people who had been there before avoided Ned. But every month, there were some newcomers who didn't know about Ned's reputation or some regulars who were too slow in diving for cover, and he would launch his assault.

Ned wasn't genuinely interested in anyone or anything other than Ned. Ned was bored by other people, and other businesses, unless they were potential customers for NedCo. Of course, he couldn't understand how or why anyone would *not* want to be a NedCo customer. After all, NedCo was the most fascinating thing he could think of. And besides, he *really* needed more sales. So Ned just pushed harder.

There were others like Ned. They circled like sharks around a ship, waiting for someone to jump in the water. If a newcomer showed up, they attacked.

Over time, a funny thing happened to the networking event: NetPlus people stopped coming to it. They felt like they were prime steaks at a meat market, or the hottest electronic gadget at a Black Friday sale. Ned, and those like him, descended on them like pigeons on a stray french fry at a picnic. The NetPlus people didn't get enough value from coming to make it worth their time. It was a NetMinus event for them.

Without any NetPlus people, the event was full of the Neds. They circled around each other, shaking hands, slapping backs, and laughing with phony guffaws. They probed for weaknesses in each other's defenses, launching their elevator speeches, shoving business cards and brochures, and pinning each other down for lunches for the following Tuesday.

Eventually, even the Neds stopped coming, and the event died.

Let me be clear: I believe that great things can happen at networking events. I like going to good networking events. In fact, I organize a few of them myself, many of which have roughly the same format as the one in the story above. But a good networking event has ground rules, and the first rule is this: *Don't Be a Ned.* Ned-like behavior kills an event, because it reduces networking to nothing but a meat market, and potential connctions to merely sales prospects. Don't get me wrong: we all hope that our networking results in sales, and if an event never produced any sales then it's just a cocktail party or a conference. But good business is the natural outcome of positive relationships, built on mutual respect, trust, and interests. When we try to jump past respect, trust, and mutual interest and just push for the sale, we alienate people who value the other qualities. And who values them? NetPlus people. The meat market approach will merely drive away the NetPluses, leaving you with a room of NetMinus Neds, trying to sell to each other.

We all need customers, clients, and contacts. But NetPlus connections aren't commodities. They are earned, not acquired.

To illustrate the problem, consider dating. If you go to places or events looking to "score" without building relationships, you will alienate quality men and women. You can go to bars or clubs and try to "hook up" without taking the time to get to know people. But good, long-term relationships don't begin in places like that. If you take the time to build positive relationships, love might result. But look for love without relationship, and you'll miss both. My purpose here is not to give dating advice, but to make the point that relationships, of any kind, cannot be reduced to mere transactions.

We all need customers, clients, and contacts. But NetPlus connections aren't commodities. They are earned, not acquired. You cannot sweet talk, cajole, push, bully, or wear down NetPlus people. Not because they are indestructible supermen or superwomen, but because they have enough smarts and self-respect to walk away from a NetMinus that has them cornered. They may take the business card and nod their head for a few minutes, but the NetMinus should not expect a call. Nor should the NetMinus pester them with calls, because it won't get him anywhere. NetPlus people are valuable, and they are interested in and attracted by value.

My suggestion: if you go to a networking event, go to listen and learn more than to talk and sell. Be valuable, offer valuable advice, and help however you can. Make introductions, and be open to suggestions. That, more than anything else that you or the brochure you brought along might say, will attract the attention of the NetPlus people at the event. And connecting with NetPluses will result, long term, in bigger and better sales than you would have gotten by being a Ned.

• • •

"Let no one ever come to you without leaving
better and happier."
— Mother Teresa

Chapter 11

Better How?

NetPlus people not only make everyone else's world bigger, but *better*. How do they do this?

That's really a two-part question. First, *in what ways do other people's worlds get better?* By what measure are they improved? Second, *by what means do they bring about these improvements? Let's take those questions one at a time.*

Better in Which Ways?

"Better" is, of course, a subjective concept. We all want to make more money, and if we are responsible to a manager or for employees, we need to produce enough income to meet those responsibilities. So the obvious answer would be that NetPlus people help us make more money.

But "more money" is not as simple of a concept as it might at first seem. A NetPlus person might improve our world by buying our product, or helping us to sell it to others. He or she might also improve our bottom line by helping us to be more efficient or open us to productive new ideas. To make more money might first require getting out of unprofitable situations, such as cutting back on people, or shutting down an endeavor. Making more money in the long term might even mean making less in the short term, by dropping things with limited potential and investing in growth.

Because NetPlus people authentically want to help, and are interested enough in the world to have explored it and gained some wisdom, they bring valuable perspective to our challenges. They can help us sort out the differences between wants and needs, short and long term goals, and what is truly profitable and sensible.

And money shouldn't be our only motivation or metric. Right now, you could make more money by putting down this book and taking a second or third job. It might be something that you hate doing, but you would be getting paid for your time. However, these extra few dollars might come at a terrible cost to your family, health, or other values you hold dear. In the long run, compromising those things might even cost you more money if your life and other businesses collapse.

A NetPlus person brings genuine solutions to meet your *real* needs. It is important to remember the difference between needs and wants. At one time or another, most of us lose sight of what would be best. We want things that we may not need, and which might actually prove harmful to us in some way. But because NetPlus people are genuinely motivated to help others, and are interested enough in the world to have explored it and gained some wisdom, they bring valuable perspective to our challenges. They can help us sort out the differences between wants and needs, short and long term goals, and what is truly profitable and sensible.

A NetPlus vendor or salesman doesn't just push superficial products to satisfy immediate wants. He or she learns what we need and proposes solutions that go deeper and further to meet our business challenges. A NetPlus employee sees the gaps in our business model, or what is breaking down in our execution and may be costing us money, and helps to fill or fix them. A NetPlus colleague gives good advice, steers us away from unproductive and unprofitable mistakes, and points us toward solutions we might have missed.

NetPlus people also genuinely care about the welfare of others. Randy Bednarz is an engineer for my company, Quantum Leap. He takes care of our clients' telecom issues, gremlins, and outages. One day, Randy responded to a call where the client's telephone system was struck by lightning (a common occurrence in the spring). When Randy arrived on site he noticed the transformer had melted a bit, and the system would need to be replaced.

While Randy was assessing the damage, a young man walked into the room to hear his diagnosis. Randy noticed a little blood coming out of the young man's ear. Randy asked, "Were you outside when the lightning struck?" The young man nodded. Randy was immediately concerned. To be safe, he strongly urged the young man to go to the hospital and get checked out. He resisted but ultimately agreed to go. This young man was the son of the owner of the company. His father ended up writing Quantum Leap a grateful email, thanking Randy for his persistence in urging his son to go to the hospital. The doctors had determined that the lightning traveled through his body and into his head. He began to lose his hearing, and there were other complications that they were able to treat. He remained in the hospital for a few days for additional care. Randy's genuine concern for others made a significant difference in this young man's life.

Because NetPlus people are great business allies, we often see the results in our personal lives, as well. Fewer problems and better opportunities mean less stress and more time to devote to other things that matter to us. Because they introduce us to other NetPlus people and the bigger world around us, we enjoy our work more and accomplish our non-monetary goals. NetPlus people are catalysts, combining and multiplying the elements of success in our professional lives. Our professional worlds literally improve because we have them around us. They make us better at what we do, and better able to enjoy it.

How Do They Do It?

As we've pointed out several times, NetPlus people don't *do* NetPlus, they *are* NetPlus. It isn't a set of techniques, but a pattern of character, habits of mind, and lifestyle. That being said, I have noticed that there are at least five ways that NetPlus people seem to go about improving other people's lives.

1. **They genuinely want the best possible outcome for everyone involved.** Whether they are organizing a business deal, leading a team or a production line, organizing a conference, or helping to resolve a dispute, NetPluses don't try to create winners and losers. They are experienced enough to know that not everyone can win or get everything that they want all the time, but they work toward constructive, not destructive,

solutions. They are not always relentless do-gooders (they can be the most successful and relentless negotiators), but they are not motivated by professional malice, nor are they callous toward other people's pain and loss. They are realistic optimists, and believe that some good can come out of every situation. They intuitively work to bring that about intuitively, which is why they are so often change agents for improvement.

They don't keep score. NetMinus people don't really help other people, they trade favors. They aren't genuinely interested in making someone's world better, but in putting someone in their debt so they can collect later.

---

2. **They listen and learn before they speak.** NetPluses are smart enough not to express an opinion about a situation until they understand it. They don't propose inappropriate products or services at unrealistic prices, because they take the time to do their research before they make their proposal. They learn what the people around them are thinking, feeling, needing, and wanting *before* they offer solutions. They are good matchmakers, because they don't make introductions or connect connections without first getting to know the

parties involved. Because they are genuinely curious about and interested in the world around them, listening is not a chore. They want to know more than they want to talk.

3. **When they do talk, they are honest.** NetPluses don't have hidden agendas. That doesn't mean that they don't have personal agendas, or aren't trying to achieve for themselves or their employers, but they don't hide their interests, or pretend to be something that they are not. All of us are justifiably suspicious and cautious in business, because there are so many people we cannot trust. Some of us have even become cynical, believing that no one tells the truth, and that we are always getting played. Again, NetPluses have agendas and pursue what is profitable to them, but there is no deception in it. When they make a proposal or give advice, it is honest. This makes a better world for the people they deal with, who can make a fair and rational decision about whether their interests and the interests of the NetPlus are in alignment. Aligned interests move parties toward cooperation and shared wins.

4. **NetPlus people have had enough success themselves to become shrewd.** We've all heard the old saying, "Physician, heal thyself." It's hard to take a proposal or advice seriously if the person making it hasn't had any success with it in their own career. Either it doesn't work, or the

person proposing it hasn't tried it himself. NetPlus people have had enough success with whatever it is that they are proposing to know what they are talking about. They propose appropriate solutions, or give sound advice, from experience. They have been there, and done that. They improve other people's worlds by zeroing in on the real issues, and recommending what has been proven to work.

5. **NetPluses don't keep score.** NetMinus people don't really help other people, they trade favors. They aren't genuinely interested in making someone's world better, but in putting someone in their debt so they can collect later. That might improve my world, but at a cost. Don't get me wrong: I'm not saying that NetPluses freely give away their products or services. A worker is worth his wages, and honest business is profitable. When NetPluses sell something, they don't resent undercharging and then try to manipulate or use guilt to get what they want. A sale is a sale, and a deal is a deal. The NetPlus makes a better world for clients, contacts, and colleagues by giving and expecting fair value, and preserving respect and trust between the parties.

Conclusion

You want NetPluses all around you, because they will make your professional world better with what they do and how they do it. In fact, they will make you better at what you do, so that you get more than a one time, short-term improvement in your world. As catalysts for positive change, they will put your professional world on a path of continuous improvement, and help you to become a catalytic NetPlus for others. This is not just altruism. NetPluses know that a rising tide lifts all boats, and that if they can create a successful culture around them, it will be mutually profitable to everyone they are connected with.

• • •

"I expect to pass through life but once. If therefore, there be any kindness I can show, or any good thing I can do to any fellow being, let me do it now, and not defer or neglect it, as I shall not pass this way again." — William Penn

Chapter 12

Twelve Ways NOT to Network

NetPlus people make the professional worlds of the people around them better. They certainly don't make them worse—that's NetMinus territory. Just as we defined "better" in the last chapter, it's worth listing some of the ways that we can make the networking experience worse for those we meet.

To be clear, there are a lot of ways that you can make someone's world worse in the networking process. You could spill red wine on their shirt at an event. You could offend them with an inappropriate joke, or go on for an hour at dinner about your recent deer hunting trip. But these kinds of errors fall under the general file of "people skills," and if you lack those, then successful networking is out of your league and is probably the least of your problems.

Instead, let's look at some of the specific ways that you can make people uncomfortable in the process of meeting and connecting with them. To state the obvious, if they are uncomfortable with you from your first interaction, the likelihood of future interactions drops dramatically. So, to keep you from becoming a Ned at your next networking event, here are twelve things a NetPlus networker would never do.

1. Do not try to close before connecting.

NetMinus networkers follow Alec Baldwin's advice in the movie Glengarry Glen Ross: "A.B.C. Always. Be. Closing." I could introduce you to people who follow that advice, and make a lot of money. Of course, as soon as I introduced you they would be trying to close a sale with you. The "A.B.C." Rule violates the Golden Rule, "Do unto others as you would have others do unto you." Off the top of my head, I can think of a half dozen people who are always closing before they make a genuine connection with someone, but I can't think of a single person who wants to be on the receiving end of that. People might succumb to this technique everyday, just like people succumb to being assaulted on the subway. No one likes it, and once they figure out what's happened to them (which, I admit, can take some time), they will no longer trust you and you'll have no follow up sales. But if immediate sales are your only goal, then it can and does work. In contrast, NetPluses make solid connections before trying to sell, much less close. They know that over the course of a long term business relationship there will be far more opportunities, sales, and profit than can ever come from a hit and run attack.

2. Do not *rely* on marketing collateral.

I am a huge believer in effective branding and well-done marketing materials. But business cards, brochures, and other marketing handouts are only tools to help facilitate making connections, they don't make connections on their own. I cringe whenever I see people at a networking event shoving materials into people's hands before establishing rapport or building the ground floor of a professional relationship. I always have business cards with me, but I am not too quick to pull them out. I'd rather talk first, and get to know the other person. I prefer to learn who they are, what they do, who they know, and how their business is going. I let them ask me about myself before I volunteer any information. Usually, I don't have to push my card on them, they ask me for it. As for brochures and any other material, they only come out if my new contact requests it. In fact, I often will bring those sorts of things to our second meeting, or mail it. I never let marketing materials about me or my business become a crutch or substitute for getting to know someone, and learning about their interests.

3. Do not smell of desperation and fear.

I have been through some tough times in my career, when my back was against the wall and my company was in real danger. I know what it's like to be under enormous financial and other sorts of pressures. In those times, it's all that you can think about. But please hear me: if you let that show on your face, in your body language, or through your actions, it will drive a stake through the heart of your networking efforts. New contacts can smell your desperation and fear. Without even thinking about it, they will pull back. Our instinct for self-preservation subconsciously programs us to avoid someone in trouble. It takes strong morals, courage, compassion, and training of the will to jump into the water to rescue a drowning person. And while I believe we all are willing to help someone in trouble, we don't want to be put in that position at a networking event. The point of making new professional contacts is to communicate our value, not our neediness. If you are desperate and afraid in your business right now, you will unintentionally cycle between asking for pity and pushing too hard to make a sale. Both will backfire, and brand you as a NetMinus. If that's where your business is right now, then you need to get people you trust to help you formulate a plan to get on solid footing, and guide you through a rebuilding process. But don't run around networking like a hysterical character in a disaster movie.

4. Do not be obnoxious or unattractive.

I don't mean physically unattractive. Most successful people don't look like models or actors. But you should look professional, well groomed, and composed. You don't have to wear latest designer labels, but dress appropriately for the industry and the event. Keep your shoes shined and clean, buy a new shirt and tie or skirt, blouse and jacket. Stains on your clothes practically scream for attention in a meeting—look into a full-length mirror in the light before you leave the house. You may have two different color socks or shoes on and not realize it. Presentation and first impressions can make or break the deal. We once interviewed someone who was wearing an extremely white wrinkled shirt. During our team deliberation we quickly disqualified "the wrinkled shirt guy" because he seemed not to care about his image. Show respect and project yourself as someone that others would want to meet. Develop your basic business manners and people skills. This is not complicated: in a room full of people sizing each other up, make a good first impression. Make them want to meet you, and when they do, make them want to have a follow up meeting.

5. Do not be a phony.

Don't pretend to care about someone or something when you don't, because people can detect it, and you will lose far more points than you potentially would have gained. Don't pretend to be someone that you're not, or more important than you really are. No one likes someone who puts on airs, wildly exaggerates, or flat out lies about their career or background. Phonies, or people who are good at faking it, make all sorts of contacts and develop all sorts of connections. But they are playing a dangerous game. Eventually, their network figures them out and they become a laughingstock. That's why con men always have to find new targets.

6. Do not have a bad reputation.

Your professional reputation is your brand equity, and once it is squandered it takes a lot of effort to rebuild it. Networking is about people making introductions, and if you are known to be trouble—for past business mistakes or for being a NetMinus person—they will not introduce you to their NetPlus contacts. I have been at plenty of networking events where I have heard colleagues warn each other about someone who was more trouble than they were worth. Unfortunately, sometimes this devolves into unfair gossip. But beyond gossip, a bad track record will make it very difficult to make new connections. If you have that kind of reputation in your community or industry, then you need to address it right now. In this short space I can't cover all the possible problems and solutions, but get a trusted and experienced business advisor and follow her advice.

Twelve Ways NOT to Behave at Networking Events:

- Do not try to close before connecting.

- Do not rely too much on marketing collateral.

- Do not smell of desperation and fear.

- Do not be obnoxious or use vulgar language.

- Do not be a phony.

- Do not have a bad reputation.

- Do not ask for inappropriate favors.

- Do not be too enthusiastic about the networking process.

- Do not violate professional distance.

- Do not be socially blind and deaf.

- Do not push solutions in search of a problem.

- Do not sell lemons.

7. Do not ask for inappropriate favors.

Professional boundaries are not clearly marked, and the rules of professional courtesy are usually unwritten. But that doesn't mean that they aren't there, and if you step over or break them, even unintentionally, you risk losing a potential connection. The person you meet might be a NetPlus, and may genuinely want to help you out. But don't put them in an awkward situation by asking for something that they did not offer or cannot give. For example, a friend of mine who writes books and speaks around the country is constantly being asked to read people's unpublished manuscripts, or to pass on their resumes, or to meet personally with them to give advice. He is a generous NetPlus with genuine concern for others, but he simply does not have the time or energy to meet all of these requests. If he met even a quarter of them, he couldn't get his own work done. Often, people he has just met at an event corner him (metaphorically and sometimes literally) and dominate his time so that he cannot meet others. People are understandably enthusiastic fans, and want to take the opportunity to learn what they can from him. But you will get further with new contacts, even NetPlus contacts, if you respect professional boundaries. Let someone *offer* to meet with you, or make an introduction for you, or read your resume or manuscript.

8. Do not be too enthusiastic about the networking process.

Some people really get so into the game that they forget the objective. I meet people that seem to do nothing but go to networking events, or collect new contacts on LinkedIn or Facebook. They treat making connections like scoring points. But that's *not* the point. The point of meeting people and connecting with them are the opportunities it creates. Collecting names and numbers does nothing for you unless you cultivate those relationships so they bear fruit. I'd rather have fifty really good connections than five hundred that are shallow and pointless.

I also meet people who look forward to networking events as social gatherings. I also enjoy the events, but I don't go for entertainment or social validation. I go to meet interesting people, so that our worlds become bigger and better. The networking event isn't a high school dance, or a nightclub.

9. Do not violate professional distance.

We've talked about relationships throughout this book. Please remember that I mean *professional* relationships. There are boundaries between our professional and personal lives, and while some business relationships develop enough to cross that boundary, they don't start out that way. In networking, you cannot assume familiarity that the other person hasn't granted. A new contact's family life, religion, even their hobbies, are off-limits to conversation unless *they* bring it up. That doesn't mean that you should volunteer that information about yourself, unless social cues indicate that you have permission. If I've just met you at a professional networking event, I don't want to hear about your faith, your weight loss journey, your childbirth experience, your messy divorce, or your money problems. I don't want to be invited to hang out with you and your spouse at the beach next weekend, or for drinks with your friends on Friday night. Maintain professional courtesy and distance until you have permission to become more intimate.

10. Do not be socially blind and deaf.

In the last point, I said to maintain professional distance until you have permission to become more intimate. But how is that given? No one comes right out and says, "Let's take our relationship to the next level and be friends." Like animals, humans have a complex, non-verbal language. In fact, studies indicate that the vast majority of what is communicated between humans is non-verbal. We "speak" through body language, tone of voice, facial expression, etc. To understand what is being communicated in a networking situation requires seeing and hearing the non-verbal content of the conversation. And even that depends on context, so we need to be hearing and seeing what is going on around us in the conversation as well. If you are blind and deaf to social signals and subtle messages, you will stumble through some meetings and miss other opportunities. We must be sensitive to not only what is being discussed, but what is being said, when meeting new contacts.

11. Do not push solutions in search of a problem.

Sometimes, we have a product or service that we have to sell. Perhaps we have to sell it because it's our job to do so, perhaps we genuinely believe in it and feel compelled to see it succeed, or maybe we desperately need to close sales for financial or personal reasons. Whatever the case, sometimes we promote a solution before we have uncovered a problem that it can solve. When we do, we reverse the sales process, which involves discovering a need and proposing a solution that can meet it. At every networking meeting I go to, I see people promoting a company or a product for which there is no evidence of demand. It reminds me of going to a crowded marketplace in a developing country and watching a vendor hawking trinkets to the tourists. Every now and then someone stops to buy, but it's a low-percentage, hit-and-miss game. Better to make an introduction, learn about the other person's business challenges and opportunities, and only *then* propose solutions that would address their needs. If that means that they don't need the product you are selling, then introduce them to someone who does offer the right solution. Then you would be then practicing NetPlus connecting.

12. Do not sell lemons.

Sometimes, you are selling something that simply doesn't work, or doesn't work well. It might be your job to sell it, but you will never get far building professional networks as the representative of an inadequate product or service. If that's your current situation, then the next chapter is for you.

• • •

"Everyone thinks of changing the world, but no one thinks of changing himself."
— Leo Nikolaevich Tolstoy

Chapter 13

Selling Lemons

We all have a job to do, and honor and honesty demand that we do our best for our employer. We should be deserving of our wages, or quit taking them. If our job is to represent the company to customers, suppliers or the general public, then we should do so with loyalty and enthusiasm. I have no "ifs, ands, or buts" to add to that statement.

However, I do have a follow up question. What if you come to realize that the company, product, or service you represent doesn't meet its customer's needs, or fails to provide the value they paid for? Why am I asking this in a book about building NetPlus connections? As you build networks, your connections should begin to think of you in terms of your employer or set of solutions. This creates two dilemmas for the NetPlus person.

First, since the NetPlus person's whole orientation is to make other people's worlds bigger and better, how can she make connections while knowing that her work is *subtracting* value from her clients? Second, as people realize that she is selling something that is itself a NetMinus product, won't they come to see her as a NetMinus person? How can a true NetPlus initiate connections to deliver something that costs more than it's worth?

This goes to the heart of the NetPlus philosophy. How we think about the problem of having to "sell lemons," much less what we do about it, may very well determine if we are really NetPlus when the going gets tough, or just when things are so good that it's easy to be a nice person.

These are not hypothetical questions. At one time or another in our career, lots of us have had to work for, represent, or sell something that we knew wasn't a winner. We have seen the flaws in our own system or solution, and listened sympathetically to customer complaints. Many of us have realized that our competitor has a better mousetrap. Especially in recent years, with a weak economy, many of us have had to take jobs working for something that we didn't really believe in.

This is a real test for the NetPlus person, and it's worth discussing because it goes to the heart of the NetPlus philosophy. How we think about the problem of having to "sell lemons," much less what we do about it, may very well determine if we are really NetPlus when the going gets tough, or only when things are so good that it's easy to be a nice person. There are at least four issues that you must face if you find yourself having to"sell lemons."

Honesty

A lawyer's job is to represent his client's interests and position as well as possible. You do not expect a lawyer to give you an objective, third-party evaluation of their client. If the lawyer did that, it would be professional misconduct. A client pays his attorney to be his advocate, to portray him as positively as possible within the boundaries of the truth. In this sense, a salesperson is like a lawyer: her job is to advocate for the product or service they are selling, within the boundaries of truthfulness. But what happens if selling the product or representing the employer requires lying to a customer? Or even allowing falsehoods to stand in the customer's mind? In that situation, the NetPlus person has a tough decision to make. To whom do they want to be a NetPlus asset: the dishonest employer, or the deceived customer? They cannot be both.

Authenticity

We all need to make a living, and that means taking the field wearing the uniform of the company writing our paycheck. But if that company stands for values that are not our own, then we need to ask ourselves whether it matters to us if we are authentic in our professional life. Is this job making you into someone that you are not, or into someone that you don't want to be? Can you live with your colleagues believing you to be someone other than your true self? There are plenty of great companies and products that I might not be personally passionate about, but which I could still represent without having to pretend that I'm someone I am not. But if I had to live a professional lie in order to make a living, I hope that I would find another way. Which brings me to integrity.

Integrity

Look at the word *integrity*. It's related to words like *integrate* and *integral*. It means that all the parts of something fit together, are in alignment and in harmony with each other. If my personal and professional values, as well as my relationships with customers, colleagues, and employer are all out of alignment with each other, I have lost my integrity. The parts of my life no longer fit together and I am not functioning as a whole and consistent person. Building a network to promote poor solutions to my connections disintegrates me. And if my world is not integrated, I cannot be trusted, and I certainly cannot build NetPlus connections.

Longevity

Will the people you value stick with you if you sell lemons to your connections? I'll say it again: we all need to make a living, and in a weak economy any of us might have to take a job just to support our family. But if a job is costing us our honesty, authenticity, and integrity then we are no longer NetPlus people. In fact, it could cost us our long-term career. Not only will selling lemons make us develop a bad reputation, we will no longer have the rich, deep networks that are the hallmark of NetPlus people. Without those networks, we cannot make other people's worlds bigger or better, and ours will become smaller and worse. Where do you want to be, and whom do you want to know, in ten years?

As we wrestle with these four issues, we have to confront two practical questions.

1. Can we improve our company, product, or service?

If it's not right or goes against your principles, can it be fixed? Do you know how? Do you have the influence and the opportunity? Do you have the endurance, or skill sets, to be a change agent? How much opposition will you face? Is it worth it to try? There are so many variables to these questions that all I can do is to encourage you to get advice and coaching from wise and experienced people around you.

2. What are your career options?

If it were possible to just go to work for a better company in the same industry, I assume that you would do that. Let's assume that you do not have that option, for whatever reason. Then you have to ask yourself if you want to stay in an industry that is forcing you to become a NetMinus person. Is it time to find some other way to make a living as a NetPlus? Is this job worth what it is costing you? Do you have the courage to try?

It seems like these days I meet more and more people who don't like their work, or the product or service they offer, or how they are treated in their business. It must be difficult for them to go to work every day with these types of challenges. As hard as it is to find work right now, I believe there are opportunities available for everyone who desires change. As you think about what you're offering others in your business, or as you consider the current culture where you work, are you in a position to be a NetPlus person?

> *If my personal and professional values, as well as my relationships with customers, colleagues, and employer are all out of alignment with each other, I have lost integrity. The parts of my life no longer fit together, and I am not functioning as a whole and consistent person. Building a network to promote poor solutions to my connections disintegrates me.*

I try to be proactive, and listen to personal development CDs every day. Some are so good that I listen to them over and over again. One of my favorites is Jim Rohn. Jim has some great advice for those of us that want to get more out of life and how not to settle with our jobs if we aren't happy and want "more." More could equal a lot of things: more money, more time with our families, more time off, a better life. In one of Jim's talks, he argues that there are winds all around us, which are blowing all the time. What we need to do is set a better sail to catch that wind to carry us to our destination or our goal. You see, some people believe that they are stuck in their job and there is nothing they can do to change their position. They blame the reason they are a NetMinus person on their circumstances, their job, or their boss. Jim and I emphatically disagree. The wind is there for all of us—we just need to set a better sail. A better sail might be training for the position you want at your company, or going back to school to get your degree, or participating in a network marketing business part-time to help you gain control of your circumstances and make more money. Maybe it's finding a better job online. The point is that you can either be a NetMinus person, blaming others and imagining yourself as a victim, or you can become a NetPlus person and live the life you deserve.

• • •

"We make a living by what we get, but we make a life by what we give."
— Winston Churchill

Part IV

Value Attracts Value

Chapter 14

Show Me the Money

I regularly meet people who misunderstand the purpose of NetPlus. Usually, they say something like,"I think that helping people is great. But I'm in business to make money. If I wanted to do good works, I'd volunteer for a charity. How does making other people's worlds bigger and better make me richer?"

I understand their confusion. We are not taught to think this way in most business courses or books. Most of the people who speak and write about success focus on setting financial goals and overcoming any obstacles that stand in the way of achieving them. They encourage us to develop our motivations for and visualization of business success to a sharp edge, and let that cut through any resistance in our world. NetPlus, on the other hand, encourages you to be motivated by helping others to solve their problems and achieve their dreams. Throughout the first three sections of this book, I've reminded you again and again that you should focus on making everyone else's world bigger and better.

We do not need to choose between pursuing profit and making other people's worlds bigger and better. NetPlus people do both. In fact, the point of NetPlus is to make your business profitable by means of improving the lives of others.

So, as we begin this final section of the book, let me set the record straight about a few things:

1. I am in business to provide a living for my family, myself, my employees, and any charities or other people I choose to help—in that order.

2. I like money, and I work hard to make as much of it as I can for the list of people above. I don't feel guilty about that. In fact, I'm proud of my accomplishments.

3. I use my time and resources as productively as possible to turn as big of a profit as I can.

However, I also believe the following:

4. If I make it my business to make other people's worlds bigger and better, it will have the effect of increasing the value of my world as well.

5. As my professional world becomes more valuable, it will be reflected in my financial bottom line. A bigger and better professional world will mean a bigger and better bank account.

To avoid any possible misunderstanding, let me say as clearly as I can that NetPlus is not a "do-gooder" system, but recognition of a fundamental truth: value attracts value. Valuable people are attracted to other valuable people, and in the same way NetPlus people find each other. As we go through our careers and make the thousands of "relational balance sheet" assessments, the cream rises to the top. That doesn't mean that the people at the top of every organization are the best people—our own experience and the news teach us that incompetents and crooks can rise very far indeed. But the best people do succeed in ways that matter. They win awards, they build successful businesses, they are asked to serve on boards, and they make good money. They are also respected, and have lives that others admire and emulate. And as they meet and make connections, they introduce each other into their "club:" the informal fraternity of the NetPluses.

Being admitted into this group is a great honor. It means that you are valued. And you get there by always being worth more than you cost to the people are around you.

Ah, some of you are thinking, *this is what I was afraid of. I don't want a pat on the back, the respect of my peers, nor do I want to be asked to serve on committees. I want money. Ken, you're still dodging that issue!*

But I'm *not* dodging the issue. This objection is still missing the point because it assumes that we must choose between pursuing our own profit as our primary goal or working to make other people's worlds bigger and better. But this is not an either-or dilemma. NetPlus people do *both.* In fact, the point of NetPlus is to make your business profitable by means of improving the lives of others.

Imagine you are a kid again, and you are going to start a lemonade stand in front of your house on a hot summer day. You could focus exclusively on your goals, but your business would never get bigger than the amount of energy you could invest in it. You might hire some neighbor kids, but they would just be employees because they have no stake in the outcome beyond what you pay them.

Or, your goal could be to make a lot of money for yourself *by making everyone in the neighborhood's world bigger and better.* You would produce great tasting, cold lemonade that really cooled people off on a hot afternoon. You would serve it well, and price it so it was a great deal. You would make your stand a hub of activity, and make introductions between neighbors who didn't know each other well. You would learn what other needs the adults had, beyond thirst. You would get the other kids involved by finding out what they could do well, and plugging them not only into the business, but into the other adults. For example, you might discover one neighbor kid down the street who knew how to trim shrubs, and match him up with the elderly lady around the corner whose yard needed some work. You might introduce the girl next door to the family on the next block who needed someone to feed their cat and bring in their mail when they go out of town. All the sudden, you are making the neighborhood a bigger and better world—not to the exclusion of your lemonade business, but in the course of running it. You and your lemonade stand are adding all sorts of additional value. You've become NetPlus. And you are almost certainly making great money doing so as your customers recognize your value.

NetPlus is for business people who are smart enough to realize that the surest path to success is to be valuable to everyone you connect with.

There have been great heroes of industry—Thomas Edison, Henry Ford, Bill Gates, Walt Disney, Steve Jobs— who became successful beyond anything they could have imagined because they added value to everyone's world. They gave us light, or transportation for the ordinary family, or entertainment, or technology for the masses, or computers that changed the way we lived. Our world is bigger and better because of their relentless efforts to provide products and services that were worth more than they cost, and their ability to build and sustain large organizations that deliver them. And the value they gave reflected back on them. They were NetPlus assets to the marketplace, and it rewarded them richly.

NetPlus isn't for "do-gooders" (although it is for people who want to do good). It is for business people who are smart enough to realize that the surest path to success is to be valuable to everyone you connect with.

● ● ●

"It's not that successful people are givers; it is that givers are successful people." — Patti Thor

Chapter 15

In Defense of the Business Lunch

Every now and then I hear someone say that business should be "all business," with no fluff or wasted time.

It's true that the heart of business is a basic transaction, which doesn't require a relationship between buyer and seller. For example, last night I ordered a new piece of luggage from Amazon.com. I wanted a specific brand, item, and color, and couldn't find it in any local stores (I did look around). Since I'm leaving for a trip next week, I went ahead and found it online. Thirty seconds and a few clicks later, it was on its way. All business, no relationship required.

Technology is making these kinds of transactions easier. Relationships can be time-consuming, expensive, and messy. Focusing on the transactional part of the business cycle is far more efficient and predictable.

The problem with that approach is that the relational part of the cycle never goes away. True, there was no relationship required for me to order my new bag last night. But there were a lot of relationships involved in the total business cycle that surrounded my purchase. There were relationships involved in the design and manufacture of the product. There were relationships involved in marketing the product, by the manufacturer and Amazon. There was a relationship between the manufacturer's representative and my local stores, which decided not to stock this particular item. There were relationships inside Amazon that were required to efficiently sell and ship the product quickly. I have relationship with my bank, which helps me run my business and provides the credit card I used to place the order. And I wanted the new bag for the business trip I'm taking next week to visit some clients and colleagues. In fact, there is a giant web of professional connections that surround my thirty second click-click purchase. To focus on that transaction and argue that modern business can eliminate the expense and risk of building relationships is to ignore the vast relational infrastructure that makes my quick purchase on my smart phone possible.

> *Much of what is communicated between human beings is non-verbal. Essential qualities like trust, compatibility, alignment of interests can only be determined by face-to-face meetings.*

At the core of the business relationship is trust. Trust is essential, even in an online purchase: I trust that Amazon will not overcharge my credit card, that they will ship the item on time, and that it will be as described, etc. I trust Amazon because of my prior experience and the experiences of millions of other customers, which are reflected in their user reviews. But if I don't have prior experience with a person or company, and I cannot easily check references with a large number of their other customers, I have to forge that trust. This requires establishing some sort of professional relationship. That might involve verifying documents and calling references, but most of the time it takes meeting the people involved to "size them up."

Much of what is communicated between human beings is non-verbal. We evaluate people based on how they appear, their body language, the tone of their voice, eye contact, how they carry themselves and react in certain contexts. We can't get much of that through writing. Every day, I meet people through email and start a dialogue with them. But a dozen positive email exchanges with a new connection can be undone by five minutes with them in person. Phone calls are a little better because we can learn a lot by someone's tone of voice and manner of speaking, but that's still a limited bandwidth of information.

We might collect resumes and sort candidates via email, or set up an initial meeting with someone through an online dating site. But none of us would hire an employee without an interview, or commit to a relationship without a series of dates. Essential qualities—like trust, compatibility, and alignment of interests—can only be determined by face-to-face meetings.

The vast machine that makes that single transaction possible is lubricated by human contact. NetPlus people not only remember that, they master it.

That's why I don't let my employees just sit in an office and email our suppliers and customers. Especially if it's a new connection, and even more so if there is a problem. At a bare minimum, they must get on the phone and call them, but that's only if a face-to-face meeting isn't possible. If there are any questions in the professional relationship, my rule is for my people to get over to see them, bring them here, or let's meet in a neutral location. Let's look them in the eye and figure out how we can do more and better business together.

All our communications technology has made it too easy to avoid those kinds of meetings. Yes, sometimes a quick email or text message can save time by transmitting some non-controversial information. I just got an email from Amazon saying that my order has been shipped, and giving me package tracking information. One of my customers just sent me a text message asking me to send him some information. I forwarded the text to someone on my staff that will take care of it. But I have some accounts receivable that are past due, and some suppliers that haven't sent me what they promised. Emails are not enough. Someone on my staff, maybe me, needs to sit down and work through whatever the problem is.

If you ever get the opportunity to meet my sales team (some of you have), ask them what we do. They all answer the same way: "We help people." Because isn't that what we are all really here to do in life and in business, to help people? Of course the next question is, "Help people with what?" My staff is all trained to ask their connections three questions: *What is going well for you? What's not going that well? And what's a goal you have for next year?* How the contact answers those questions gives us a roadmap toward making their world bigger and better.

When our team fails to hear back from a prospect, what do they do? They either find a lead for that prospect's business, or help that prospect in some other way. They might solve another problem in their business, or help a member of their family. Their goal is to find some other way to make that person's life better because they met us. You can't do that with much success through social media like Twitter or LinkedIn. It's about personal connections.

We have the communications technology to work with anyone, anywhere. But because business relationships involve establishing rapport and trust, and so much communication is non-verbal, using distant suppliers and collaborators does not always work as well as we hope it will in the digital age. We have to take the measure of the people we are working with, forge alliances, and understand how they think. We need to learn what their interests and goals and capabilities actually are, in comparison to what they advertise. Video conferencing works when we are discussing facts, but feelings don't come through the screen. If our business connections are far away, someone usually needs to get on an airplane, often more than once.

And so, I not only defend the business lunch, I defend the business dinner, the industry conference, and even the business golf outing. Not with every customer or supplier or colleague, and certainly not to the exclusion of getting the transactional part of the business cycle done. But the vast machine that makes that single transaction possible is lubricated by human contact. NetPlus people not only remember that, they master it.

• • •

"More business decisions occur over lunch and dinner than at any other time, yet no MBA courses are given on the subject." —Peter Drucker

Chapter 16

Career Karma

One of my favorite movies is *It's a Wonderful Life,* because it illustrates one of the fundamental truths of the NetPlus approach to professional relationships.

Because it's one of my favorites, and a classic film, I often make the mistake of assuming that everyone has seen it. If you haven't, watch it! Until you do, here's a brief summary.

Released in 1946, it tells the story of George Bailey (played by James Stewart) in the fictional town of Beford Falls. The film begins with George considering suicide on Christmas Eve. He runs a savings and loan bank in Bedford Falls, and due to an unfortunate error (it wasn't his fault) the institution is severely overdrawn. He faces arrest for bank fraud, and the collapse of everything he has built in his life. Standing on a bridge, he tries to convince himself that his life insurance policy makes him worth more to his family dead than alive.

His family and friends begin praying for him, and Heaven sends a guardian angel to help George put his life into perspective. To everyone in Bedford Falls, George has always been what we are calling a NetPlus person. The angel helps him recall how, from childhood how he repeatedly put other people's interests ahead of his own.

He put off going to college until his younger brother Harry could graduate from high school and take his place in the family savings and loan business. But circumstances forced him to stay and run the business, and he generously gave his college savings to Harry, sending him off in his place. On his wedding day, during the Great Depression, there was a run on their bank. To prevent the collapse of the savings and loan (and the loss of all the townspeople's assets), George and his wife Mary deposited their honeymoon money into the company accounts to keep them liquid and cover their customers immediate withdrawals.

Over the years, George generously assisted the working poor of the town to build and own homes with affordable loans. He had an opportunity to take a high-paying job with a bigger bank, which would allow him to travel to places like New York and Europe. But the family business and the people of the town needed George, and he let his brother Harry take the position instead. When World War II broke out, he couldn't enlist because of an injury he incurred while saving Harry's life when they were children. George spent his life investing in his brother, and Harry went on to become a fighter pilot hero, winning the Congressional Medal of Honor.

Everyone whose world George had made bigger and better over the years responds in his hour of need, making him realize how big and great his world really was.

George spent his life making the people of Bedford Falls' world bigger and better, but he becomes despondent, believing that he has nothing to show for it. The people have homes, his brother has fame and success, but George has never seen the world or gotten rich. He is stuck in his home town, running the family business, and trying to make ends meet. The banking error threatens the savings and loan with total collapse and George faces arrest unless he can come up with enough money to cover the bank's obligations. He decides that his NetPlus approach has led him to failure and ruin.

But his guardian angel keeps him from jumping by showing him the value he has brought to the town and everyone he has worked with over the years. And when the townspeople learn that George's business is in a debt crisis, they respond. They flood his home, bringing in small donations of cash from their coffee cans and mason jars. A distant colleague that George had helped over the years wires a large line of credit to the bank. Everyone whose world George had made bigger and better over the years responds in his hour of need, making him realize how big and great his world really is. The savings and loan, and more importantly George's life and the well being of his family and town, is saved.

Because he chose to build a bigger and better world, he got to live in a bigger and better world. Because he was a NetPlus person, other NetPlus people were loyal to him. Value attracted value.

One evening this past summer as Barbie and I visited some friends at their lake cottage in northern Michigan, I shared the story from *It's a Wonderful Life* with my nephews, nieces, and five preteens as a pre-bedtime story. I shared it with energy and passion, not missing an important scene to keep up their interest and engagement. They asked questions about the story and were curious about some of the decisions George made and the difficulties he had as a result. As I got to the end, a few of the older kids were moved by the outpouring of love that the townspeople showed to George. My niece Olivia and our friends' son Brendan were both very impressed with the story and couldn't wait to watch it on TV. They loved the fact that I planned on sharing how much this story impacted my life and how I planned on including it in my NetPlus book. Over the next two days they both began suggesting titles for the book, and for the next three weeks Olivia sent me quotes to put in my book because she believed they were relevant and she desperately wanted to help me. Here is one quote she sent me in email: *"A generous man forgets what he gives and remembers what he receives." There will be lots more coming Uncle Kenny!!!!!!! :)"* I appreciate and love her so much. Children can inspire us to do so much if we will just take the time to tell them stories and listen to them.

It's a Wonderful Life also illustrates one of the ways this value-to-value exchange happens, something I call "Career Karma." As I've said before, as NetPlus people go through life, they don't just fit into the existing culture, they proactively create a value culture around them. They raise standards, they inspire and connect people, and they learn and teach others. NetPlus don't just make other people's worlds bigger and better, they make others into bigger and better people, and organizations into bigger and better organizations. George's guardian angel shows George an alternate reality: what Bedford Falls would have been like if George had never lived. In that alternative history, it was a cruder, meaner place, and the people who George knew and loved were less noble and unhappier.

The concept of "karma" is that the deeds we do affect the trajectory of our future. It serves as a great way to think of the consequences of our professional choices; what goes around comes back around, as they say. If we go through our career making NetMinus choices—making other people's worlds smaller and worse—not many will show up in our hour of need with cash from a mason jar to rescue our business, like they did for George Bailey. We reap what we sow, or fail to reap what we fail to sow.

NetPlus people don't go through life doing favors to put people in their debt, like a politician or a mafia boss. George Bailey had no expectation that the town would rally to his side because of his innumerable decent acts over many decades. George also did not try to run his business as a charity. He tried to run a successful business that would thrive by doing the right thing, improving and enlarging the world around him. It would miss the point to say that his career karma "paid off," because he never thought of it that way. But because he chose to build a bigger and better world, he got to live in a bigger and better world. Because he was a NetPlus person, other NetPlus people were loyal to him. Value attracted value.

NetPlus: it's a wonderful life.

• • •

"He has the right to criticize who has the heart to help." — Abraham Lincoln

Chapter 17

Reproduction

NetPluses don't just make other people's worlds bigger and better, they make more NetPluses.

When I think of adjectives that describe NetPlus people, words like generous, connected, and secure come to my mind. Those qualities give them a drive, like a biological impulse, to reproduce themselves. They share their gifts with the world, and love to invest in other potential NetPlus individuals around them. They are relational creatures, wanting to know more people so their network of connections can always be growing. And they are not threatened by having others around them who are successful and might become better at some things than they are.

Much of this is instinctive and impulsive. NetPluses don't have to remind themselves to impart their innate characteristics to others. It's a matter of influence; throughout their career, more NetPlus people appear in their wake. But as we near the end of this book, I want to talk about a more deliberate reproductive act: the training of apprentices.

An apprentice is not just an employee or assistant, or a colleague that you share ideas with. It's not a deputy or a vice president. Nor is an apprentice an intern, a low-paid, entry level position. As I am using the term, an apprentice is someone that you are deliberately teaching to do what you do, in the way that you do it. It means working intentionally with them to help them to become like you. In other words, to reproduce yourself.

Religious leaders, great artists, philanthropists, and pioneers of big, new ideas have always known that the best way to spread their message is to infuse it into a small number of disciples and send them out into the world.

I'll say more in a few moments about how to make apprentices, but some of you might be wondering why you should bother. After all, as we said above, aren't you already influencing other people to become NetPlus? Don't you already have employees that you are training and supervising? Doesn't apprentice-making require a lot of time and effort that could be more productively spent? And isn't it sort of egotistical, an act of narcissism, to believe that the world needs more of you? Let me give you three good reasons why you should be training apprentices.

First, it's just smart organizational leadership. Do you lead an organization? Are you vital to that organization? If you answer that last question with, "No, not really," than I suggest you ask yourself why you are not. There are two reasons why you might not be vital to the organization you lead. You could be superfluous, and bring no unique skills to the position. If so, then you need some professional and leadership development. On the other hand, if it's because you've empowered others and have built a self-sustaining organization, then you have probably already been making apprentices for some time. Great leaders reproduce themselves so that the organization continues to grow and thrive while they focus on strategy and new initiatives.

Second, making apprentices is a strategic career move. Mentoring others who can do what you do and turning them loose makes your world bigger and better. It gives you intimate connections throughout your industry. Through your apprentices that have "left the nest," your influence is multiplied to people and organizations two and three connections removed from you. Expanding your network through apprentices that have gone on to become successful themselves creates unforeseeable opportunities in the future.

Finally, making apprentices is proof that you're serious about what you believe. If you are really committed to your values, ideals, and causes, then building them into apprentices increases the impact your beliefs can have on society. Religious leaders, great artists, philanthropists, and pioneers of big, new ideas have always known that the best way to spread their message is to infuse it into a small number of disciples and send them out into the world.

So, how do you go about training apprentices? There are entire books and workshops on the mentoring process, and I cannot adequately summarize such a vast subject here. However, for our purposes, here are a few things I have learned over the years.

1. Start by asking yourself, "Who around me has the potential to do what I do?"

This might be obvious, but it's harder to practice than you might think. We are all unique, a complex mixture of nature and nurture. One of the biggest pitfalls in training apprentices is to try and force a square peg into a round hole. There might be people around you who can learn to do some of what you do, and you should be teaching them, but true apprentices are people who are capable of seeing what you see and doing what you do in the way that you do it. Trying to force someone into your mold when it isn't natural for them will only result in frustration and failure for you and your attempted apprentice.

2. Let your apprentice surpass the master.

As you train an apprentice, he or she may come to see more than you see, and be able to do more than you can do. There is a fine line between reproducing yourself and stifling someone else's creativity and capabilities. Even though I keep saying that the goal is to reproduce yourself, the truth is that an apprentice something like having a child. You give them your professional "genes," you raise them within your business family, you transmit your values, and then you release them grow and become their own person. They will always carry you inside of them, but they may accomplish more than you. That is a good thing.

3. Don't try to have too many apprentices at one time.

Really, unless you are exceptional in this regard, most of us can only have one, or at most three, apprentices at any one time. The apprentice needs your time, access to your thinking, and the ability to follow you around and watch what you do. You cannot have an entourage and be really building anything meaningful into them.

From the beginning, the whole relationship is focused on the day when the apprentice leaves to become a master practitioner of his own. Therefore, apprenticeships should not last one day longer than they have to in order to achieve that goal.

4. Apprenticeship is not book learning or classroom training.

You might have students, but apprentices are not students or interns. An apprentice works alongside his master, listening to his thoughts, learning not only what he does but why he does it a specific way. An apprentice emulates his or her master. He takes in a thousand subtle things about how the master lives and works, and then incorporates them into his own life. This cannot be done through sessions in a classroom or office by a master "teaching." Because of this, apprenticeship is a very serious and deliberate investment of time by both parties.

5. The goal is not to *have* apprentices, it is to *release* them.

Do not mistake means and ends: there is no point in having apprentices for their own sake. From the beginning, the whole relationship is focused on the day when the apprentice leaves to become a master practitioner of his own. Therefore, apprenticeships should not last one day longer than they have to in order to achieve that goal. It might take three months or three years, but do not take on an apprentice if what you really want is an assistant or a flunky.

6. Consider how taking on an apprentice will affect the non-apprentices around you.

Giving this level of extraordinary access to one person could raise questions about fairness and lead to jealousy. Others who have worked hard and are ambitious will wonder why they do not have the same opportunities that your apprentice does. Some of that might be jealousy, but not all of it. You need to ask yourself whether you are being fair to others. One of the biggest mistakes you can make in taking on apprentices is to unconsciously surround yourself with "yes men," people that don't challenge your thinking. By definition, they are not really NetPlus anyway, because they don't add value. Are you avoiding others in your organization with great leadership potential because they might force you to grow yourself?

7. Don't reproduce your bad habits.

Reproducing yourself is a great idea, if you are reproducing your positive qualities. But teaching someone to do what you do in the way you do it can be a

KEN FORTIER

double-edged sword: they could pick up your faults and foibles. And you do have faults and bad habits, just like the rest of the human race. A master-apprentice relationship can backfire by multiplying your dysfunctions. Use the time you spend with your apprentice challenging yourself to improve so that you give them the best of yourself.

I am blessed to have such an amazing team of individuals at Quantum Leap. The team has expanded over the years from one (me) to twenty-four (at present). Of course there has been some turn-over along the way. We have tried—and anyone who has led a growing organization knows how difficult it is to pull off—to cherish and protect the culture of the organization as you add people over time. Nothing worth having in life is easy, but I have had the pleasure and privilege of hiring and partnering with some special individuals over these past nine years, and I have appreciated each and every employee, even if we decided that Quantum Leap was not a good fit for their future.

But when I think of apprenticeship, one team member in particular stands out. His name is Mike Borowka. Mike joined my team in 2005. His mom Marcia was my banker at that time. She asked me if I knew of any opportunities available for her son who wanted to find a sales position. I met with him and offered him a job. He was the first salesperson I had ever hired at Quantum Leap. Mike's background was in recruiting for the University of Phoenix in Arizona and as a golf pro for Kent Country Club. He really didn't know much about telecom but was eager to learn. During those first six months, Mike shadowed me and was coached by the person who had mentored me. He went to meetings with me, and participated in the Junior Achievement program. I could see a bright future for Mike because of his commitment and hard work. He was conscientious and a connector, a great potential NetPlus. Things were moving along fantastically. Then one day, Mike walked into my office and closed the door. He was frustrated because, in his opinion, he wasn't performing as well as he thought he should, and so he had found another job at a local professional recruiting company. He shared how bad he felt because he wasn't producing, and he didn't want to strain the company. I asked him if he could give himself three more months. I saw something in Mike, and I believed he was close to hitting his stride and didn't want to see him go. I decided I would spend more time with him and help him get some wins.

Three months turned into six years, and now I'm proud to share that Mike is the President of Quantum Leap Communications. I believed in Mike and I have a great deal of respect for him. He is the perfect apprentice who challenges me when it's appropriate, he cares for the team as much as I do, and has as much compassion for kids and the community as I do. If you all could be so fortunate to have an apprentice grow to a level where you could trust without question to hand over the keys to your business, your team, your project, you will realize that achievement is truly remarkable.

Right now, are you reproducing yourself? Are you making more NetPluses, not just accidentally but deliberately? Who are you raising up within your organization to replace you so that you can grow yourself and take on new challenges? Do you have a plan, and are you taking deliberate steps to train apprentices and release them to become masters themselves?

• • •

"Surround yourself with the best people you can find, delegate authority, and don't interfere as long as the policy you've decided upon is being carried out."
— Ronald Reagan

Chapter 18

Who's Who?

I wrote this book because I wanted to share a philosophy that I believe in and has served me well. I also wanted to give you a vocabulary, a way to talk about your professional relationships that articulated what you may have always have felt but lacked the words to describe.

But most of all, I wanted to help you to become a NetPlus asset to the people around you, or to become more of one if you already are. I wanted to show you how you can create a bigger and better world for the people around you, creating more value for you, them, and all of us. Hopefully, some of what I've shared in this book will help you to do that.

Which brings us back to where we started: the relational balance sheet that all of us keep, whether we admit it or not. NetPlus is based on the premise that some professional relationships cost more than they are worth, and some are worth more than they cost. How much of our resources and opportunities we invest in people depends on that evaluation. It can be painful, it can be liberating, but it is always real. The impact we make with our career will largely depend on whether we invested wisely for maximum return. Avoiding this kind of relational accounting doesn't make the issues go away. If we are to create a "value culture" around us, we must ask the tough questions about ourselves and those that we work with.

You have finite resources and opportunities to spend on your professional relationships. But remember that some of those are fixed overhead costs, which you cannot use for discretionary spending. You can't spend everything at work.

WHO'S WHO?

That's what this chapter is about: I want you to make an inventory of your professional connections, asking which ones are NetPlus assets and which are NetMinus liabilities. Who's who?

As you do so, please remember to keep the following points in mind.

1. What matters to you?

Every professional relationship has some costs and brings some benefits. Every balance sheet lists assets and liabilities. But while the *concepts* on our balance sheets are the same, the *particulars* might (probably?) differ. What aspects of a relationship do you consider to be a cost, and which a benefit? Let me give you a simple example.

For me, preparing a meal for someone else is a cost. I don't necessarily avoid it, anymore than I would avoid any other chore. If that's what I need to do, I'm happy to do it. But it's not a benefit of the relationship. If I have a friend or guest, I might consider *eating* the meal with them a benefit, but not the *preparation* of it. If I enjoyed eating it with them enough, the experience would be worth it. But I have a friend who loves to cook for people. Whether it is for family, friends, or colleagues, cooking is a life-giving experience for her. It gives her joy, and the process of preparing a meal—not only eating it—is an act of love and a reward in itself. She and I both have relational balance sheets, but cooking would be on the liability side for me and on the asset side for her. The principle activity is the same, but the particulars are different.

So, as you ask who's who on your sheet, you need to decide what your values, joys, frustrations, burdens, and benefits are. That means that someone who is a NetMinus for me might be a NetPlus for you. But be honest with yourself. The point of this inventory is for you to really assess your professional relationships and decide where to invest. Don't feel pressured into calling a NetMinus a NetPlus on your sheet if it's not true. That will get you nowhere.

2. Don't forget your overhead costs.

You have finite resources and opportunities to spend on your professional relationships. But remember that some of those are fixed overhead costs, which you cannot use for "discretionary spending." So, for example, your family deserves a certain amount of your time, money, energy, etc. If you are religious, so does God. And you need to invest in yourself. I don't mean that in some selfish, narcissistic way, but if you don't make time to sleep, exercise, eat right, and refresh your mind and spirit, you will have nothing left in the tank for others. You have to maintain yourself, like you would maintain a crucial piece of equipment, so it is available to serve others. These fixed overhead costs need to be built into your balance sheets. You can't spend everything at work.

> *Let me share this from the bottom of my heart: always give the benefit of the doubt, and error on the side of generosity of spirit. I don't know how you think about these things, but I will find it easier to stand before God someday and say that I was always as graceful as I could possibly be.*

3. Calculate costs and benefits over time.

Just like anything else in business, costs and benefits are not evenly distributed over time. There are phases in a business cycle when you are spending more than you are bringing in. Whether you are building a new home, launching a business, or expanding with a new project, sometimes it seems that all you are doing is writing checks without getting any immediate or apparent return on the investment. Obviously, that can't continue forever. But it's only common sense that you sometimes invest for a season to reap a later return. As you evaluate who's who on your relational balance sheet, I encourage you to remember that someone might be costing you more than they are worth at the moment, but that it might only be for a season. Conversely, they might have benefited you greatly in the past, and thus have a great deal of accumulated equity in your books. Look at the full cycle of the relationship.

4. When in doubt, error on the side of grace.

Sometimes these judgments are easy, and sometimes they are very difficult. What if someone is "on the bubble?" What if the costs and benefits more or less cancel out? Let me share this from the bottom of my heart: always give the benefit of the doubt, and error on the side of being generous and forgiving. I don't know how you think about these things, but I will find it easier to stand before God someday and say that I was always as graceful as I could possibly be. If that means that now and then I give someone one too many chances, or "write off" a few extra costs in a relationship, so be it. I can't afford to do that endlessly and still use my time and opportunities well, but I will gladly give up a few percentage points of effectiveness to be kind, good and give everyone around me as much of myself as possible.

I encourage you to make this inventory. Do it right now. Take a sheet of paper (destroy it afterward), and be honest with yourself. It is the beginning of investing yourself to the best of your ability in a bigger and better world for everyone.

WHO'S WHO?

• • •

"There is no use whatever trying to help people who do not help themselves. You cannot push anyone up a ladder unless he is willing to climb himself."
— Andrew Carnegie

Conclusion

Now What?

I began this book by pointing out that technology has enabled our professional connections to grow a mile wide and an inch deep. We are electronically "connected" to hundreds, or thousands, of contacts that we barely know and interact with only in the most superficial of ways, spread out across the country and globe.

There is nothing wrong with these social media connections, as long as we don't mistake them for actual professional relationships. From the dawn of time, business has always involved intangible elements—trust, rapport, understanding, alignment of interests—that could only be cultivated by direct interaction. Whether in trade, academia, politics, or religion, human endeavors have always advanced through relationships and alliances. We forge these alliances through direct engagement and shared experiences, which requires investing time, resources, and opportunities in each other. We cannot count on people that we don't really know.

Figure out what is keeping you from being as valuable as you could be to others, and make it as small a part of your life as possible. Recognize what about you blesses and encourages and enriches others, and make that the biggest part of your life.

NetPlus people make a bigger and better world for everyone around them by being worth more than they cost. In these pages we've explored the what, why, and how of that equation. We've also seen what happens when it gets turned upside down, and people become NetMinus liabilities by costing others more than they are worth. You may not have agreed with everything you read in these pages, but I hope that this book has been valuable, a NetPlus investment of your time and money.

If so, then now what? How can you put down this book and put its principles into practice today? To conclude, let me offer six immediate suggestions.

1. Decide that you will be a NetPlus person from this point forward.

Yes, you will have to learn to work hard to implement these ideas, but all of that begins with a simple decision: will you do what it takes for your professional contacts to consider you an asset? Will you strive to always be worth more than you cost? At its core, NetPlus is an orientation of the mind, a way of seeing and thinking about how you relate to other people. Do you first seek to serve, or to be served? Is your first reaction to find fault and cast blame, or to solve problems and be a catalyst for positive change? What's in your heart? What are your default habits of mind and behavior? What will you accomplish with your career, and what will you be remembered for? Forget who you've been, who will you *become?* You can make that decision right now, before you finish this page. It might take a lot of work to bring it about, but decide now whether you will move to the right or to the left, towards NetPlus or NetMinus.

2. Make a rigorous self-assessment, commit to what is valuable, and leave behind whatever isn't.

We all have some thinking and behaviors which place extra costs and burdens on those around us. None of us are perfect, and we never will be. We can't eliminate our faults, but we can minimize them. But before we can do that, we have to recognize and acknowledge what they are.

As I said earlier, one of the biggest problems with NetMinus people is that they don't realize that they are NetMinuses. Can you see yourself as others see you? This can be painful, because we all have self-defense mechanisms that keep us from looking too closely in the mirror. If we can't be honest with ourselves, we are doomed to repeat our failures over and over. Figure out what is keeping you from being as valuable as you could be to others, and make it as small of a part of your life as possible. Recognize what about you blesses and encourages and enriches others, and make that the biggest part of your life.

3. Mend your fences and build some bridges.

We've all made mistakes and hurt people along the way. We all have some strained relationships and some rough edges on our reputation. That is what is dragging behind you, slowing down your career. It limits your connections, and makes your world smaller and worse. And if your world is smaller and worse than it could be, there are limits to how much bigger and better you can make someone else's world. If there are relationships that can be fixed, fix them. If there are NetPlus people you have withdrawn from because something went wrong, then reach out. If your reputation has been tarnished, clean it up. I'm not suggesting that you go back to every boss that ever fired you, to every teacher that ever gave you a bad grade or every coach that ever cut you from a team. But if your name can be restored, start rebuilding. If there are any hurt feelings that could be cured, then offer salve to the wounds. If there are any closed doors that could be opened with an apology, then knock. Make things right, so that you have a surplus of connections and opportunities to share. This is a challenge, directly from my heart to you. I believe every relationship can be mended. No matter how damaged. Make this day a new beginning for you and take the first step to clear your heart. Be genuine, look them in the eye, and tell them, "I was wrong and I am sorry." In fact, write to me at ken@netplusconnections.com and share your experience. I'd love to read about your successes, as well those attempts at reconciliation that don't work out. Maybe it's not the right time for them, and so try again soon.

4. Think bigger, but act smaller.

Small thinking can make us NetMinus people. If our minds are full of little thoughts, little hurts, little ambitions, and little rivalries, we become little people. We won't be able to make anyone else's world bigger, because ours is so small. NetPlus people think big: they see the big picture, they are plugged into the bigger world around them, and they are connected to bigger networks of people. But big thinking can lead to big problems: grandiosity, arrogance, and elitism. Some NetMinus people are so enamored with the forest that they can't see the trees, much less accomplish anything of practical value. True, NetPlus people think big, but their behavior is characterized by practical action. They can think at the 30,000 foot strategy level, but they can also accomplish things on the ground. They aren't just dreamers and idealists; they can focus on implementing the details. NetPlus people know how to delegate, but they don't just push all the execution off onto others while their heads stay in the clouds. They have big ideas, but they get the small things done. So dream, but don't just dream, do. You will become immensely valuable to everyone around you.

5. See what's wrong, and imagine what could be better.

NetPlus is not a positive thinking scheme. NetPlus people are not just optimists, who see the glass as always half full and think only happy thoughts. They are practical, tough-minded people. They don't ignore problems, they identify them. They are fully aware of what is not working, of needs and injustices. They intuitively grasp the flaws in a system or proposal. But they are not pessimists, critics, or naysayers. NetPlus people may point out problems, but only so that they can propose solutions. They don't dwell on the problem side of the equation, because once that's been identified they are already imagining how it can be made better. Decide today that from this point forward you will be a practical optimist. You will be realistic about the present, but your eyes will be focused on a better future, and you will be helping everyone around you to bring that about.

Together, we will be NetPlus assets to our colleagues, our connections, our communities, and our country. Ultimately, we will be assets to our world, making it more peaceful, positive, and prosperous. We will all win, and be happier and wealthier because of it.

---

6. Create, and enjoy, a culture of value.

Give more than you take, help more than you hurt, and be worth more than what you cost. If you let those principles shape how you work with others, you will not only be valuable, you will make everyone around you more valuable. You will have influence, and contribute to a culture of value. Everyone will have a bigger and better world. You will be part of the solution to every problem, and surrounded with opportunities you never imagined. You will enjoy reaping what you sow.

• • •

I look forward to connecting with you, either directly or indirectly. Together, we will be NetPlus assets to our colleagues, our connections, our communities, and our country. Ultimately, we will be assets to our world, making it more peaceful, positive, and prosperous. We will all win, and be happier and wealthier because of it. But it begins with us. Let's be NetPlus connections to everyone we work with from this day forward.

I believe that we all have the potential to be NetPlus. The power of NetPlus is in all of us, we just haven't put into action as much as we should. My hope is that these principles and this book are the push you needed to get started and do something new and great that you didn't do yesterday. Right now, look through your list of connections and pick three connections that are NetPlus assets in your life. Call them, take them to lunch or dinner, and ask them what's going well for them. Ask them what's not going well. Ask them what their goals are for next year. Listen to them with genuine interest. You will then have your opportunity to become a NetPlus asset to them: figure out how to help them by making their world bigger and better.

I hope that you realize that this book has been an invitation to join the NetPlus community. I'm on your side, and I hope that you will contact me and help me spread the message and invite more people to be worth more than they cost. Sow these NetPlus philosophies, and reap the reward of value attracting value. Who knows?

NOW WHAT?

Maybe one day soon we'll meet and help each other. Wouldn't that be remarkable!

• • •

"Know Thyself." — Socrates

About the Author

Ken Fortier is the CEO of Quantum Leap Communicaitons, a telecommunications and electrical business in Grand Rapids, Michigan. In a few short years, Ken's company has grown from an idea to a thriving and profitable business providing value to over four thousand clients. He is also the founder of the consulting firm NetPlus Connections, training others to become the most valuable professionals they can be. He lives in West Michigan with his wife Barbie and their two children. To learn more, please visit:

www.netplusconnections.com

• • •

Greg Smith is a writer and speaker. He works in a variety of genres across a wide range of topics, frequently collaborating with other authors. He is the owner and chief creative officer of Black Lake Studio & Press in Holland, Michigan, where he lives with his wife Linda and their two children. To learn more about Greg, please visit:

www.smithgreg.com

Page 191